FRAUD AUDITING AND
FORENSIC ACCOUNTING

FRAUD AUDITING AND FORENSIC ACCOUNTING

New Tools and Techniques

G. JACK BOLOGNA, B.B.A., J.D.

Assistant Professor of Management
Siena Heights College
Adrian, Michigan

ROBERT J. LINDQUIST, B. COMM., C.A.

Partner
Peat Marwick Lindquist Holmes
Toronto, Ontario

JOHN WILEY & SONS

New York · Chichester · Brisbane · Toronto · Singapore

This publication is designed to provide accurate and
authoritative information in regard to the subject
matter covered. It is sold with the understanding that
the publisher is not engaged in rendering legal, accounting,
or other professional service. If legal advice or other
expert assistance is required, the services of a competent
professional person should be sought. *From a Declaration
of Principles jointly adopted by a Committee of the
American Bar Association and a Committee of Publishers.*

Library of Congress Cataloging in Publication Data:

Bologna, G. Jack.
    Fraud auditing and forensic accounting.

    Bibliography: p.
    1. White collar crime investigation—United States.
2. Forensic accounting—United States. 3. Fraud
investigation—United States.   I. Lindquist, Robert J.
II. Title.

HV8079.W47B65   1987   363.2′5   87-21025
ISBN: 0-471-85412-3

Printed in the United States of America

10 9 8 7 6 5 4 3 2 1

PREFACE

Writing a book is not something one does for ego gratification or monetary reward. Indeed, most books provide authors very little fame or fortune, and a book for a limited audience of technical specialists provides an even more modest return on effort. So why do authors take on such enormous tasks for such little reward?

Such books are most often written out of a compulsion to share a few professional insights and anecdotes with professional colleagues who appreciate one's lifelong interests. Indeed, that was our primary purpose.

Our goal in writing this book was to make a contribution to the literature in the fields of auditing, investigation, and forensics. Beyond that, we hope that our work stimulates an awareness of the meaning and value of fraud auditing and forensic accounting.

This book deals with deceptions of many kinds but mainly of an accounting nature. Deception undermines our faith in people. It makes *all* a little poorer, not merely the victim. So whereas we may speak of deceptions of all manner in this book, we hope not to destroy faith in people but to reduce the temptations in our society and in organizations that cause and foster deception of an accounting nature.

Accordingly, this book is intended neither as a formula for financial deception nor for fraud detection, because there is no successful formula for either.

Deception and its detection are qualitative things—not quantitative. They are mainly states of mind.

Deception deals with human character or, more properly, with the lack thereof. Character is a mental thing, a matter of personality and upbringing. Detection deals with a mind-set too; a mind-set that suggests that truth, justice, and fairness in human relationships and business transactions are important values and ought to be preserved and promoted. It is to that end that we commit this book.

In the broadest terms possible then, this book deals with the growing international problems of white-collar crime from the perspective of how such crimes can be investigated and documented by forensic accountants, how they can be detected by internal and external auditors, how they can be investigated by police and security authorities, and how they can be prevented and deterred by good management practices.

White-collar crime does not create the public fear or concern that street crime does. Yet a recent report by the Joint Economic Committee of the U.S. Congress states that street crimes produce yearly losses of about $4 billion, whereas white-collar crimes may cost U.S. citizens over $80 billion annually. In terms of dollar loss alone, one might question society's permissive attitude toward white-collar crime.

Our dichotomous perspectives on street crimes and white-collar crimes are based mainly on media coverage. The media tend to concentrate reportage on street crime, and unless a political figure, a social lion, or an economic giant is involved, the media tend to overlook white-collar crime.

If our role models (economic, political, and social leaders) are corrupt, greedy, or inept, can we realistically expect their subordinates to behave much better than they do? Imitation of superiors is one way we all learn. If our superiors value honesty and therefore behave honestly, we tend to mimic that behavior. If, on the other hand, they behave dishonestly, the need for fraud auditors and forensic accountants is created.

So it is to the fraud auditors and forensic accountants of the world that we dedicate this book. But we cannot leave the subject of dedication without recognizing the sacrifices made by the spouses of fraud auditors and forensic accountants, especially the sacrifices made by our spouses, Angela Lindquist and Jean Bologna. Their loyalty, strength, and support during our many days and nights away from home allowed us to keep our minds firmly committed to our task.

And to Barbara Davis, Pat Kobold, and Ann Graham, a special thanks for the kind care they showed for our every word, phrase, and illustration. Their dedicated services as advisors and typists have earned them a special place in the heaven of fraud auditors and forensic accountants.

G.J. BOLOGNA
R.J. LINDQUIST

Plymouth, Michigan
Toronto, Ontario
June 1987

CONTENTS

INTRODUCTION

Why a book on fraud auditing and forensic accounting at this time by these authors, a Canadian practicing public accountant who specializes in forensic accounting and an American management generalist who specializes in the design and delivery of skills training for managers and in organizational development? Does the world really need another book on human greed and deception? Haven't these topics been exhausted by now?

The foregoing questions were posed to us by friends, colleagues, and publishers when we first proposed to do this book. You may be asking those questions yourself. So let us attempt to clarify our intentions by explaining why the book was written and for whom, what benefits readers might derive from it, why the book is organized as it is, and what we hope to accomplish by this combined effort.

A Canadian public accountant and an American management consultant may seem an unlikely pair to join together in any endeavor, much less the coauthoring of a book on accounting-type frauds. Yet, that may have been our original attraction. We tend to be more unalike than alike - in style, approach, and orientation. But we share a common interest in the use of accounting, audit, and investigative skills to ferret out financial frauds and solve financial crimes. Indeed, our common interest is almost a passion. We both thoroughly enjoy the challenge of preventing, detecting, investigating and documenting fraudulent transactions. So lesson one of this book is the notion that when experts agree on anything, it is probably because they share a common bias.

But, on the other hand, there are a number of good reasons why your coauthors joined together in this writing endeavor. Teaming a Canadian authority on fraud and forensic accounting with an American authority on organizational behavior has some decided advantages for readers. Our perspectives, experiences, and skills are broader and deeper. Our knowledge bases are diverse, yet stem from the same original source—the discipline of accounting—a source for each author to address the different, yet in many ways similar, subjects of fraud auditing and forensic accounting. So even in diversity there may be unity of purpose. The benefits to the reader include practical and tested techniques, sage advice, and broad perspectives.

With those as our objectives, the way to organize the book became clear to us. We first had to acquaint the reader with the field of fraud auditing in an overall sense—what, why, and how. So we call Part One an awareness of fraud auditing. When the reader completes Part One he or she will be generally acquainted with (1) fraud as a legal, social, and organizational phenomenon, (2) fraud auditing as a field of study, (3) methods to detect and deter frauds in business and (4) characteristics of organizations in which fraud is most likely to occur.

Part Two provides an introduction to forensic accounting and its investigative approach. We provide readers insight by briefly reviewing actual cases of accounting-type frauds. Here, we move from the big and broad picture of fraud to the small, or microview, that is, how the theories of fraud detection and documentation are applied in a variety of real-world cases. That way, we round out the reader's experience base and place the theories in perspective.

Part Three is designed to provide nonaccountants with a basic perspective on accounting as a discipline and the accounting field as an evolving profession that now faces the challenge of adopting itself to the expectations of the general investing public.

Celebrated cases of recent corporate and investment frauds highlight the need for an increased awareness of fraud and its manifestations in books of account, not only by accountants, but by investigators, social sciences and the general public.

The merging of the behavioral aspects of organizational fraud with the investigative aspects is, we believe, of great interest to many people at this time. It is our considered opinion that fraud and deception in business can be reduced by improving organizational cultures. So the marriage of accounting and organizational psychology in this book is, we believe, far more than just a shotgun wedding. Such multidisciplinary approaches may even be the wedding wave of the future: the marriage of the theoretical with the practical, the macro- with the microview, and the Canadian view with the American.

PART ONE

AN AWARENESS OF FRAUD AUDITING

1

WHAT IS FRAUD?

A person can cause injury to another person either by force or by fraud. The use of force to cause bodily injury is frowned on by most organized societies. The use of fraud to cause financial injury to another does not carry the same degree of culpability.

Fraud is a word that has many definitions. The more notable of its definitions are as follows:

Fraud as a Crime: The Michigan Criminal Law states:

Fraud is a generic term, and embraces all the multifarious means which human ingenuity can devise, which are resorted to by one individual, to get an advantage over another by false representations. No definite and invariable rule can be laid down as a general proposition in defining fraud, as it includes surprise, trick, cunning and unfair ways by which another is cheated. The only boundaries defining it are those which limit human knavery.[1]

Fraud as a Tort: The United States Supreme Court in 1887 provided a definition of fraud in the civil sense as:

First   That the defendant has made a representation in regard to a material fact;

Second   That such representation is *false*;

Third   That such representation was not actually believed by the defendant, on reasonable grounds, to be true;

Fourth   That it was made with intent that it should be acted on;

Fifth   That it was acted on by complainant to his damage; and

Sixth   That in so acting on it the complainant was ignorant of its falsity, and reasonably believed it to be true. The first of the foregoing requisites *excludes such statements as consist merely in an expression of opinion of judgment, honestly entertained; and again excepting in peculiar cases, it excludes statements by the owner and vendor of property in respect of its value.* [Emphasis added.][2]

Corporate Fraud: Corporate fraud is any fraud perpetrated by, for, or against a business corporation.

Management Fraud: Management fraud is the intentional misrepresentation of corporate or unit performance levels perpetrated by employees serving in management roles who seek to benefit from such frauds in terms of promotions, bonuses or other economic incentives, and status symbols.

The Layperson's Definition of Fraud: Fraud, as it is commonly understood today, means dishonesty in the form of an intentional deception or a willful misrepresentation of a material fact. Lying, the willful telling of an untruth, and cheating, the gaining of an unfair or unjust advantage over another, could be used to further define the word *fraud* because these two words denote intention or willingness to deceive.

In short, we might say that fraud, intentional deception, lying, and cheating are the opposites of truth, justice, fairness, and equity. Fraud therefore consists of coercing people to act against their own best interests.

Although deception can be intended to coerce another to act against his or her own self-interest, deception can also be intended for one's own defense or survival. Despite that rationale *for* deception, deception by current standards of behavior is thought to be mean and culpable. It is considered wrong and evil and can be excused only, if at all, by considerations of survival. But deception can be intended for benevolent reasons, too. For example, a doctor might spare a patient from learning that a diagnostic test shows evidence of an advanced state of terminal disease. Benevolent deceivers in our society are not looked upon as harshly as are those whose intentions and motives are not as pure. But deceivers who act out of greed, jealousy, spite, and revenge are not so quickly excused or forgiven.

1.1 WHY IS FRAUD COMMITTED?

Fraud or intentional deception is a strategy to achieve a personal or organizational goal or to satisfy a human need. However, a goal or need can be satisfied through honest means just as well as through dishonest means. So what is it that precipitates, inclines, or motivates one to select dishonest means rather than honest means in the quest to satisfy goals and needs?

Generally speaking, competitive survival serves as a motive for both honest and dishonest behavior. The degree of competitive threat to survival may cause one to choose either dishonest or honest means. When competition is keen and predatory, resort to dishonesty can be quickly rationalized. Deceit, therefore, can become a weapon in any contest for survival. Stated differently, it can be said that the struggle to survive (economically, socially, or politically) often generates deceitful behavior.

We could say the same about fraud in business. Fraud in business is perhaps less frequent today, but far more sophisticated. Dollar loss from fraud in business has grown exponentially. Equity Funding (see 6.6.1) alone involved overstated revenues of $200 million. The overstatement was covered up by several hundred co-conspirators who worked feverishly to generate thousands of phony insurance policies by way of company computers. Why did Equity's management persist in such deceitful practices? For survival. Unknown to stockholders and policyholders, Equity Funding was operating at a loss, despite its spectacular annual increases in volume. Telling the truth would have hastened its demise.

Beyond the realm of competitive and economic survival, what other motives precipitate fraud? Social and political survival provides incentives, too, in the form of egocentric and ideological motives. Sometimes people commit fraud (deception) to aggrandize their egos, to put on airs, or to assume false status. Sometimes they deceive to survive politically. They lie about their personal views or pretend to believe when they do not. Or they simply cheat or lie to their political opponents, or intentionally misstate their opponents' positions on issues. They commit dirty tricks against them.

Motives to commit fraud in business are usually rationalized by the old saw that all is fair in love and war—and in business, which is amoral, anyway. There is one further category of motivation, however. We call it psychotic, because it cannot be explained in terms of rational behavior. In this category we would place the pathological liar, the professional confidence man, and the kleptomaniac thief.

In addition to the motives identified above, we suggest that the internal environment of an organization can provide a climate conducive to the commission of fraud, that opportunities to commit fraud are rampant in the presence of loose or lax management and administrative and internal accounting controls. When motives are coupled with such opportunities, the potential for fraud is increased.

1.2 WHO COMMITS FRAUD?

In view of the foregoing section one might conclude that fraud is caused mainly by factors external to the individual (i.e., economic, competitive, social, and political factors, and poor controls). But how about the individual? Are some people more prone to commit fraud than others? And if so, is that a more serious cause of fraud than the external and internal environmental factors we have talked about? Data from the fields of criminology and sociology would seem to suggest so.

Let us begin by making a few generalizations about people:

1. Some people are honest all of the time.
2. Some people (fewer than the above) are dishonest all of the time.
3. Most people are honest some of the time.
4. Some people are honest most of the time.

Beyond those generalizations about people, what can we say about fraud perpetrators? Gwynn Nettler in *Lying, Cheating and Stealing*[3] offers these insights on cheaters and deceivers:

1. People who have experienced failure are more likely to cheat.
2. People who are disliked and who dislike themselves tend to be more deceitful.
3. People who are impulsive, distractable, and unable to postpone gratification are more likely to engage in deceitful crimes.
4. People who have a conscience (fear, apprehension, and punishment) are more resistant to the temptation to deceive.
5. Intelligent people tend to be more honest than do ignorant people.

6. Middle- and upper-class people tend to be more honest than lower-class people.

7. The easier it is to cheat and steal, the more people will do so.

8. Individuals have different needs and therefore different levels at which they will be moved to lie, cheat, or steal.

9. Lying, cheating, and stealing increase when people have great pressure to achieve important objectives.

10. The struggle to survive generates deceit.

People lie, cheat, and steal on the job in a variety of both personal and organizational situations. The following are but a few:

1. Personal variables
   Aptitudes/abilities
   Attitudes/preferences
   Personal needs/wants
   Values/beliefs

2. Organizational variables
   Nature/scope of the job (meaningful work)
   Tools/training provided
   Reward/recognition system
   Quality of management and supervision
   Clarity of role responsibilities
   Clarity of job-related goals
   Interpersonal trust
   Motivational and ethical climate (ethics and values of superiors and co-workers)

3. External variables
   Degree of competition in the industry
   General economic conditions
   Societal values (i.e., ethics of competitors and of social and political role models)

1.3 WHO IS MOST OFTEN VICTIMIZED BY FRAUD?

One might think that the most trusting people are also the most gullible and therefore most often the victims of fraud. Using that rationale we could postulate that organizations with the highest levels of control would be least susceptible to fraud. But in point of fact, organizations that go overboard on controls do not necessarily experience less fraud. And they have the added burden of higher costs.

Controls against fraud by either organizational insiders or outside vendors, suppliers, and contractors must be adequate, that is, accomplish the goal of control, which is cost-feasible protection of assets against loss, damage, or destruction. Cost-feasible protection means minimal expenditures for maximum protection. Creating an organizational police state is a form of control overkill. A balanced perspective on controls and security measures is the ideal, and that may require involvement of employees in creating control policies, plans, and procedures. A balanced perspective means weighing costs and benefits of proposed new controls and security measures. A balanced perspective means that a measure of trust must exist among employees at all levels. Trust breeds loyalty and honesty; distrust can breed disloyalty and perhaps even dishonesty.

Fraud is therefore most prevalent in organizations that have (1) no controls, (2) no trust, (3) no ethical standards, (4) no profits, and (5) no future.

1.4 WHY DO EMPLOYEES LIE, CHEAT, AND STEAL ON THE JOB?

The following 25 reasons for employee crimes are those most often advanced by authorities in white-collar crime (criminologists, psychologists, sociologists, risk managers, auditors, police, and security professionals):

1. The employee believes he or she can get away with it.
2. The employee thinks he or she desperately needs or desires the money or articles stolen.
3. The employee feels frustrated or dissatisfied about some aspect of the job.
4. The employee feels frustrated or dissatisfied about some aspect of his or her personal life that is not job related.

5. The employee feels abused by the employer and wants to get even.

6. The employee fails to consider the consequences of being caught.

7. The employee thinks: "Everybody else steals, so why not me?"

8. The employee thinks: "They're so big, stealing a little bit won't hurt them."

9. The employee doesn't know how to manage his or her own money, so is always broke and ready to steal.

10. The employee feels that beating the organization is a challenge and not a matter of economic gain alone.

11. The employee was economically, socially, or culturally deprived during childhood.

12. The employee is compensating for a void felt in his or her personal life and needs love, affection, and friendship.

13. The employee has no self-control and steals out of compulsion.

14. The employee believes a friend at work has been subjected to humiliation or abuse or has been treated unfairly.

15. The employee is just plain lazy and won't work hard to earn enough to buy what he or she wants or needs.

16. The organization's internal controls are so lax that everyone is tempted to steal.

17. No one has ever been prosecuted for stealing from the organization.

18. Most employee thieves are caught by accident rather than by audit or design. Therefore, fear of being caught is not a deterrent to theft.

19. Employees aren't encouraged to discuss personal or financial problems at work or to seek management's advice and counsel on such matters.

20. Employee theft is a situational phenomenon. Each theft has its own preceding conditions, and each thief has his or her own motives.

21. Employees steal for any reason the human mind and imagination can conjure up.

22. Employees never go to jail or get harsh prison sentences for stealing, defrauding, or embezzling from their employers.

23. Man is weak and prone to sin.

24. Employees today are morally, ethically, and spiritually bankrupt.

25. Employees tend to imitate their bosses. If their bosses steal or cheat, then they are likely to do it also.

Laws to be respected and thus complied with must be rational, fair in application, and enforced in a timely and efficient manner. Company policies that relate to employee honesty, such as criminal laws in general, must also be rational, fair, and intended to serve the best economic interests of the company. The test of rationality for any company security policy is whether its terms are understandable, whether its punishments or prohibitions are applicable to a real and serious matter, and whether its enforcement is possible in an efficient and legally effective way.

But what specific employee acts are serious enough to be prohibited and/or punished? Any act that could or does result in substantial loss, damage, or destruction of company assets should be prohibited.

The greatest deterrent to criminal behavior is sure and evenhanded justice, that is, swift detection and apprehension, a speedy and impartial trial, and punishment that fits the crime, (i.e., loss of civil rights, privileges, property, personal freedom, or social approval). Having said all that, why is it that despite the dire consequences of criminal behavior we still see so much of it? Apparently because the rewards gained from criminal behavior often exceed the risk of apprehension and punishment or, stated another way, because the pains inflicted as punishment are not as severe as the pleasures of criminal behavior. The latter seems to be particularly true in cases of economic or white-collar crimes.

Are white-collar criminals more rational than their blue-collar counterparts? If so, they probably weigh the potential costs (arrest, incarceration, embarrassment, loss of income) against the economic benefit—the monetary gain from their crime. If the benefit outweighs the costs they then opt to commit crime—not just any crime, but crimes against employers, stockholders, creditors, bankers, customers, insurance carriers, and government regulators.

1.5 WHAT ARE THE VARIETIES OF FRAUD?

As stated earlier, fraud is intentional deception. Its forms are generally referred to as lying and cheating. But theft by guile (larceny by trick, false pretenses, false tokens) and embezzlement are sometimes included as forms of fraudulent acts. The element of deception is the common ground they all share.

But fraud and deception are means and ends. Fraud and deception go by many other names as well. For example, in alphabetical order:

Accounts Payable Fabrication

Accounts Receivable Lapping

Arson for Profit

Bank Fraud

Bankruptcy Fraud

Benefit Claims Fraud

Bid Rigging

Breach of Trust

Breach of Fiduciary Duty

Business Opportunity Fraud

Bust Out

Cash Lapping

Check Forgery

Check Kiting

Check Raising

Collateral Forgery

Commercial Bribery

Computer Fraud

Concealment

Consumer Fraud

Conversion

Corporate Fraud

Corruption

Counterfeiting

Credit Card Fraud

Defalcation

Distortion of Fact

Double Dealing

Duplicity

EFTS Fraud

Embezzlement

Expense Account Fraud

False Advertising

False and Misleading Statements

False Claim

False Collateral

False Count

False Data

False Document

False Entry

False Identity

False Information

False Ownership

False Pretenses

False Report

False Representation

False Suggestion

False Valuation

False Weights and Measures

Fictitious Person

Fictitious Vendors, Customers, and Employees

Financial Fraud

Financial Misrepresentation

Forged Documents/Signatures

Forgery

Franchising Fraud

Fraud in Execution

Fraud in Inducement

Fraudulent Concealment

Fraudulent Financial Statement

Fraudulent Representation

Industrial Espionage

Infringement of Patents,
  Copyrights, and Trademarks

Input Scam

Insider Trading

Insurance Fraud

Inventory Overstatement

Inventory Reclassification Fraud

Investor Fraud

Kickbacks

Land Fraud

Lapping

Larceny by Trick

Loan Fraud

Lying

Mail Fraud

Management Fraud

Material Misstatement

Material Omission

Misapplication

Misappropriation

Misfeasance

Misrepresentation

Oil and Gas Scams

Output Scams

Overbilling

Overstatement of Revenue

Padding Expenses

Padding Government Contracts

Payables Fraud

Payroll Fraud

Performance Fraud

Price Fixing

Pricing and Extension Fraud

Procurement Fraud

Quality Substitution

Restraint of Trade

Sales Overstatements

Securities Fraud

Software Piracy

Stock Fraud

Subterfuge

Swindling

Tax Fraud

Tax Shelter Scam

Technology Theft

Theft of Computer Time

Theft of Proprietary Information

Throughput Scam

Trade Secret Theft

Undue Influence

Understatement of Costs

Understatement of Liabilities

Unjust Enrichment

Vendor Short Shipment   Wire Fraud

Watered Stock   Wire Transfer Fraud

Another way to view the enormity and complexity of fraud might be to design a fraud typology, as in Tables 1.1, 1.2, 1.3, and 1.4. An array of fraud characteristics may provide such insight. The lists of fraud perpetrators, victims, and fraud types are far from exhaustive. They intend merely to convince the reader that the ingenuity of man when bent on exploiting his fellow man is quite possibly unlimited. As P. T. Barnum is alleged to have said, "There's a sucker born every minute." (He is also alleged to have said, "Trust everyone, but cut the deck.")

TABLE 1.1
Fraud Typology by Corporate Owners and Managers

Victim	Fraud Type
Customers	False Advertising
Customers	False Weights
Customers	False Measures
Customers	False Representations
Customers	False Labeling/Branding
Customers	Price Fixing
Customers	Quality Substitution
Customers	Cheap Imitations
Customers	Defective Products
Stockholders	False Financial Statements
Stockholders	False Financial Forecasts
Stockholders	False Representations
Creditors	False Financial Statements
Creditors	False Financial Forecasts
Creditors	False Representations
Competitors	Predatory Pricing
Competitors	Selling Below Cost
Competitors	Information Piracy
Competitors	Infringement of Patents/Copyrights
Competitors	Commercial Slander
Competitors	Libel
Competitors	Theft of Trade Secrets
Competitors	Corruption of Employees

(continued)

TABLE 1.1 *(Continued)*
Fraud Typology by Corporate Owners and Managers

Victim	Fraud Type
Competitors	Corruption of Employees
Bankers	Check Kiting
Bankers	False Applications for Credit
Bankers	False Financial Statements
Company/Employer	Expense Account Padding
Company/Employer	Performance Fakery
Company/Employer	Overstating Revenue
Company/Employer	Overstating Assets
Company/Employer	Overstating Profits
Company/Employer	Understating Expenses
Company/Employer	Understating Liabilities
Company/Employer	Theft of Assets
Company/Employer	Embezzlement
Company/Employer	Conversion of Assets
Company/Employer	Commercial Bribery
Company/Employer	Insider Trading
Company/Employer	Related Party Transactions
Company/Employer	Alteration/Destruction of Records
Insurance Carriers	Fraudulent Loss Claims
Insurance Carriers	Arson for Profit
Insurance Carriers	False Applications for Insurance
Government Agencies	False Reports/Returns
Government Agencies	False Claims
Government Agencies	Contract Padding
Government Agencies	Willful Failure to File Reports/ Returns

Source: Adapted from Jack Bologna, *Forensic Accounting Review*, 1984.

TABLE 1.2
Fraud Typology by Corporate Vendors, Suppliers, and Contractors

Victim	Fraud Type
Customers	Short Shipment
Customers	Overbilling
Customers	Double Billing
Customers	Substitution of Inferior Goods
Customers	Corruption of Employees

Source: Adapted from Jack Bologna, *Forensic Accounting Review*, 1984.

TABLE 1.3
Fraud Typology by Corporate Customers

Victim	Fraud Type
Vendors	Tag Switching
Vendors	Shoplifting
Vendors	Fraudulent Checks
Vendors	Fraudulent Claims for Refunds
Vendors	Fraudulent Credit Cards
Vendors	Fraudulent Credit Applications

Source: Adapted from Jack Bologna, Forensic Accounting Review, 1984.

TABLE 1.4
Fraud Typology by Corporate Employees

Victim	Fraud Type
Employers	False Employment Applications
Employers	False Benefit Claims
Employers	False Expense Claims
Employers	Theft and Pilferage
Employers	Performance Fakery
Employers	Embezzlement
Employers	Corruption

Source: Adapted from Jack Bologna, Forensic Accounting Review, 1984.

Finally, fraud can be looked at from yet another perspective. When we think of fraud in a corporate or management context, we can perhaps develop a more meaningful and relevant taxonomy as a framework for fraud auditing.

Corporate frauds can be classified in two broad categories: (1) frauds directed against the company, and (2) frauds that benefit the company. In the former the company is the victim, and in the latter the company, through the fraudulent actions of its officers, is the intended beneficiary.

Frauds for the company are committed mainly by senior managers who wish to enhance the financial position or condition of the company by such ploys as overstating income, sales, or assets, or by understating expenses and liabilities. In essence an intentional misstatement of a financial fact is made, and that can constitute a civil or criminal fraud. But income, for example, may also be intentionally understated to evade taxes, and expenses can be overstated for a similar reason. So frauds for the company are usually intended by top managers to deceive shareholders, creditors, and regulatory authorities. Similar frauds by lower-level profit-center managers may be intended to deceive their superiors in the organization, to make the superiors believe that the unit is more profitable or productive than it is, and thereby perhaps to earn a higher bonus award or a promotion for the subordinate manager. In the latter event, despite the fact that the subordinate's overstatement of income, sales, or productivity ostensibly helps the company (to look better), it is really a fraud against the company.

In frauds for the organization we often find management involved in a conspiracy to deceive. In frauds against the organization there may be only one person involved in the fraud, such as an accounts payable clerk who fabricates invoices from a nonexistent vendor, has checks issued to that vendor, and converts the checks to his or her own use.

Frauds against the company may also include the bribery of employees by vendors, suppliers, contractors, and competitors. Cases of employee bribery are difficult to discern or discover by audit, because the corporation's accounting records are not generally manipulated, altered, or destroyed. Bribe payments are made under the table or, as lawyers say, sub rosa. The first hint of bribery may come from an irate vendor whose product is consistently rejected in spite of its quality, price, and performance. Bribery may also become apparent if the employee begins to live beyond his or her means, far in excess of salary and family resources.

A rough guide to classification might therefore appear as follows:

1. Frauds against the company by insiders:

   Cash diversions, conversions, and thefts, (front end frauds)

   Check raising and signature or endorsement forgeries

   Receivables manipulations such as lapping and fake credit memos

   Payables manipulations such as raising or fabricating vendor invoices benefit claims, and expense vouchers, and allowing overcharging by vendors, suppliers, and contractors

   Payroll manipulations such as adding nonexistent employees or altering time cards

   Inventory manipulations and diversions such as specious reclassifications of inventories to obsolete, damaged, or sample status to create cache from which thefts can more easily be made

Favors and payments to employees by vendors, suppliers, and contractors

2. Frauds against the company by outsiders:

Vendor, supplier, and contractor frauds, such as short shipment of goods, substitution of goods of inferior quality, overbilling, double billing, billing but not delivering or delivering elsewhere

Vendor, supplier, and contractor corruption of employees

Customer corruption of employees

3. Frauds for the company:

Smoothing profits (cooking the books) through practices such as inflating sales, profits, and assets; understating expenses, losses, and liabilities; not recording or delaying recording of sales returns; early booking of sales; and inflating ending inventory

Check kiting

Price fixing

Cheating customers through the use of devices such as short weights, counts, and measures; substituting cheaper materials; and false advertising

Violating governmental regulations (e.g., EEO, OSHA, environmental standards, securities, and tax violations)

Corruption of customer personnel

Political corruption

Padding costs on government contracts

1.6 WHAT DO WE KNOW ABOUT WHITE-COLLAR CRIME IN GENERAL?

White-collar crime is a topic much in vogue today. Seminars, symposia, and conferences on that subject abound, sponsored by government agencies, universities, trade groups and professional organizations, Chambers of Commerce, and business, fraternal, and religious organizations. Most are well attended, particularly because the cost of such crimes to individual businesses and to society is substantial. A reduction in such crimes would add greatly to corporate coffers. To appreciate the scope and nature of the white-collar-crime problem, let us review some of the literature on that subject.

The classic works on white-collar crime are *White Collar Crime*, by Edwin H. Sutherland; *Other People's Money*, by Donald R. Cressey; *The Thief in the White Collar*, by Norman Jaspan; and *Crime, Law, and Society*, by Frank E. Hartung. These authorities essentially tell us that:

> White-collar crime has its genesis in the same general process as other criminal behavior; namely, differential association. The hypothesis of differential association is that criminal behavior is learned in association with those who define such behavior favorably and in isolation from those who define it unfavorably, and that a person in an appropriate situation engages in such criminal behavior if, and only if, the weight of the favorable definitions exceeds the weight of the unfavorable definitions.[4]

In other words, "birds of a feather flock together," or at least reinforce one another's rationalized views and values.

> Trusted persons become trust violators when they conceive of themselves as having a financial problem which is nonshareable, are aware that this problem can be secretly resolved by violation of the position of financial trust, and are able to apply their own conduct in that situation, verbalizations which enable them to adjust their conceptions of themselves as users of the entrusted funds or property.[5]

In other words, "I'm not stealing; I'm just borrowing or getting even."

Jaspan's work, *The Thief in the White Collar*,[6] is based on his many years of consulting experience on security-related matters and contains a number of notable and often-quoted generalizations. In a nutshell, Jaspan exhorts employers to (1) pay their employees fairly, (2) treat their employees decently, and (3) listen to their employees' problems if they want to avoid employee fraud, theft, and embezzlement. But to temper that bit of humanism with a little reality, he also suggests that employers ought never to place full trust in either their employees or the security personnel they hire to check on their employees.

Jaspan's humanitarian generalizations are challenged by Frank Hartung, who fears that Jaspan's book ". . . may serve an end never intended by its author. . . . Sympathetic interpretation of the embezzler . . . may help to perpetuate the vocabulary of motives employed by such people since time out of mind. Their conception of *cause* constitutes, in my judgement, a *vocabulary of motives for the committing of embezzlement!* [Emphasis added][6]

Some examples of these motives described in Jaspan's work are:

1. Everyone has a little larceny in his heart.
2. Everyone has his own racket.
3. Most people will try to cheat on their income tax if they think they can get away with it.
4. Circumstances beyond their control forced embezzlers to commit their dishonest acts.
5. Mitigating circumstances were involved in the theft, such as protecting a friend, relative, or loved one who is an accomplice in the crime.

Hartung then argues:

It will be noticed that the criminal violator of financial trust and the career delinquent have one thing in common: Their criminality is learned in the process of symbolic communication, dependent upon cultural sources of patterns of thought and action, and for systems of values and vocabularies of motives.

But the career of the trust violator is quite different. First, as we said before, he is most likely not to have a previous record, even though typically he is middle-aged when detected. Second, his education, occupation, residence, friends, and leisure-time activities usually set him in a social class higher than that of the delinquent. Third, even though his crime is deliberate and he attempts to avoid detection, he fails to plan for the securing of immunity if caught. Fourth, even though he may be three or four times as old as the career delinquent, his arrest constitutes a serious crisis for him that he cannot take in his stride. His arrest and conviction and the attendant publicity are a disgrace to him.[7]

A white-collar crime, as currently perceived, is a crime committed by a person employed by a governmental or private-sector organization in a position of trust. A position of trust in this context means a position that carries authority over people and/or property belonging to another, usually property owned by an employer organization or property over which the organization has legal custody and control as an agent, bailee, or trustee. The authority vested in the position of trust carries with it certain duties, obligations, and responsibilities such as the honest, diligent, and prudent care, protection, and preservation of the property by the person in whose custody it has been entrusted. In essence, white-collar crimes involve a criminal breach of that trust, a breaking or violation of those duties, obligations, and responsibilities either by acts of commission or by omission, by overt or covert action, as in a willful fraud, theft, or embezzlement of the entrusted property, by inaction, as in oversight and neglect of duty, by negligent performance of duty, as in imprudent action and failure of judgment, or by exceeding one's legal authority.

A person in a position of trust never has carte blanche to do as he deems fitting with the property entrusted to him. Laws have been enacted to limit and regulate the nature and scope of his authority. When that authority has not been exercised prudently, the violator may be held liable, civilly. When that authority has been exceeded or corrupted, the violator may be guilty of a crime.

So the concept of white-collar crime has been broadened over the years to include not only criminal breaches of trust by people in authority roles, but breaches in business ethics as well. "Let the buyer beware," no longer carries the legal weight it once did. The seller now has obligations, too, obligations relating to fair dealing, candor, and truthfulness.

If, as many authorities claim, white-collar crime is growing rapidly and costs businesses $40 billion a year, what part of that loss is attributable to employee thefts, frauds, and embezzlement? And what part of that loss is attributable to consumer frauds perpetrated by marketers of products and services? What part of the loss is attributable to customer shoplifting? Commercial bribery? Vendor frauds? Tax frauds? Stock frauds? Unfortunately, no one knows. Even the $40 billion loss attributed to *all* white-collar crimes is at best an educated guess made by the U.S. Chamber of Commerce back in 1974. As long as we are guessing, we would venture that white-collar crime with its broader definition today costs U.S. businesses considerably more than it did in 1974, perhaps as much as $100 billion.

1.7 HOW SERIOUS IS THE FRAUD (WHITE-COLLAR CRIME) PROBLEM?

The loss from white-collar crime in general is variously estimated by United States authorities at between $4 billion and $40 billion annually. The substantial difference in opinion is attributable to the fact that there is little hard data on the subject.

In view of the scarcity of hard data on white-collar crime, we undertook a limited survey of our own. Although it is premature to make anything more than generalizations, the survey respondents—40 members of the Toledo Personnel Management Association—rank ordered in terms of seriousness and frequency of occurrence the following 25 crimes (note that two types of crime tied for first and thirteenth places):

1. Bribing political leaders
   Padding the bill on government contracts

2. Employee theft, fraud, and embezzlement

3. Pilfering small tools and supplies

4. Computer-related crimes

5. Bribing union leaders

6. Expense-account padding

7. Corporate income tax evasion

8. Stock frauds and manipulations

9. Falsifying time-and-attendance reports

10. False advertising

11. Selling mechanically defective products

12. Providing unsafe and unhealthy working conditions

13. Bribing purchasing agents
    Making illegal campaign contributions

14. Selling contaminated or adulterated drugs

15. Falsifying productivity reports

16. Falsifying company financial statements

17. Mail fraud

18. Bribing foreign officials

19. Selling contaminated or adulterated foodstuffs

20. Sabotaging company property

21. Price fixing

22. Falsifying profitability reports

23. Selling useless drugs

In terms of the white-collar crimes that would occur with greater frequency in the future, the rank ordering was as follows (note that two types of crime tied for sixth, seventh, and eighth places):

1. Computer-related crimes
2. Bribing political leaders
3. Expense-account padding
4. Bribing union leaders
5. Employee theft, fraud, and embezzlement
6. Falsifying productivity reports
   Padding the bill on government contracts
7. Corporate income tax evasion
   Bribing foreign officials
8. Stock frauds and manipulations
   Polluting the environment

How pervasive is fraud in business? And how likely is it to be discovered either by audit design or by accident? The probability of fraud in any audit environment may not be very large. If we were to speculate, we would say the probability of discovering fraud by design is about 20 percent. But we cannot support our thesis with anything stronger than impressions. A few years ago *Fortune Magazine* notated a study it did of the top 1000 industrial corporations and indicated that over a period of about 10 years 11 percent of those firms were charged with some form of accounting irregularities or corruption (i.e., commercial and political bribery, antitrust violations, tax violations, and securities violations). These were mainly in the category of frauds for the company. If we add frauds committed against those companies by their own employees, vendors, and customers, the percentage of those Fortune 1000 companies that may have experienced frauds would seemingly be higher, perhaps even double the 11 percent.

REFERENCES

1. *Michigan Criminal Law*, Chapter 86, Sec. 1529.
2. Southern Development Co. v. Silva, 125 U.S. 247, 8 S.C. Rep. 881, 31 L. Ed (1887).

3. Gwynn Nettler,*Lying, Cheating and Stealing*, Cincinnati: Anderson Publishing Co., 1982.

4. Edwin H. Sutherland,*White-Collar Crime*, New York: Dryden Press, 1949, p. 234.

5. Donald L. Cressey,*Other People's Money*, New York: The Free Press, 1949, p. 30.

6. Norman Jaspan and Hillel Black,*The Thief in the White Collar*, Philadelphia: J. B. Lippincott, 1960, p. 37.

7. Frank E. Hartung,*Crime, Law, and Society*, Detroit: Wayne State University Press, 1965, pp. 125–136.

2

WHAT IS FRAUD AUDITING?

Fraud auditing is the creation of an environment that encourages the detecting and preventing of frauds in commercial transactions. The main thrust of this book is to provide auditors and investigators with further knowledge and insight into fraud as an economic, social, and organizational phenomenon.

Investigating fraud in books of account and commercial transactions requires the combined skills of a well-trained auditor and criminal investigator. However, the combination of these skills in one person is rare, so part of our mission is to better acquaint auditors with criminal-investigative rules, principles, techniques, and methods and to provide criminal investigators with some knowledge of accounting and auditing rules, principles, techniques, and methods.

Fraud auditing cannot be reduced to a simple checklist. It is an awareness in the broadest sense of many components such as the human element, organizational behavior, knowledge of fraud, evidence and standards of proof, an awareness as to the potentiality for fraud, and an appreciation of the so-called red flags.

1. The fraud auditor should set the standard. This means that the fraud auditor within his company should have in place, and communicated to all employees, an effective corporate code of conduct that should also include conflict-of-interest policy guidelines signed by employees to provide a clear understanding of the intent of management and the level of expectations.

There should also be in agreements, especially with vendors, a clause that allows for inspection of the vendors records by the company, an inspection that can be done in the normal course.

2. The fraud auditor must have knowledge of the realm of fraud possibilities. A fraud auditor should know the types of fraudulent behavior experienced in the past and be able to relate this knowledge to the various segments of any accounting system and/or business operation. For example, knowledge of lapping in the revenue receivable receipt system.

3. The fraud auditor should know the most direct route for any investigation to follow in order to determine if substance exist to support a concern, rumor, or allegation. In the previous example, the fraud auditor should know to examine a deposit to determine if receipts from Peter are being applied to reduce the receivable balance of Paul—a quick test to indicate whether lapping is occurring.

4. The fraud auditor should look at motive and consider the environment in which the employee operates to determine if there is any possible justification. In the previous example, the manager had been placing more responsibility with this employee, which allowed the manager to take less of an interest in the company's financial well being. Two things occur in this situation: the employee is contributing more to the job than required by the job description, and, secondly, the employee notes a poor behavioral problem on the part of the manager. Together these create within the mind of the employee a position of compromise to form a motivation to steal.

5. The fraud auditor has many investigative concerns; one basic concern is opportunity. In the example, can it be shown that the person in question is the only one capable of having the opportunity to steal? Perhaps there are problems in the collection of receipts prior to the individual receiving these monies.

6. Another concern of the fraud auditor is to establish benefit and to identify assets for possible recovery. In the example, is there clear evidence that the employee is receiving a benefit? Is there a pattern of circumstantial evidence that consistently points in one direction? Is the employee living beyond his or her means? Are there any assets?

7. The fraud auditor assesses investigative findings. At various stages of a investigation, the fraud auditor must stand back and assess findings measure by the standards of proof in order to determine if there is substance to th

allegation, if a pattern of conduct exists that could suggest intent, or if the problem is simply errors and omissions in the accounting system. In the example, it may be appropriate for the fraud auditor to merely confront the employee to query Peter's money paying Paul's account. Before doing that, the fraud auditor might need to examine several transactions over an extended period of time to determine if a pattern of conduct exists and if there has been deceitful reporting to management. The assessment process is one of understanding what one presently has, understanding what may be needed, determining if there is a pattern of conduct consistent with wrongdoing, and, finally, determining if deceitful behavior exists in the employee's reporting to management.

2.1 WHO NEEDS FRAUD AUDITING?

Fraud auditing is a relatively new discipline. Whereas financial and operational auditing have long histories of acceptance, fraud auditing has come into its own only during the twentieth century, mainly with the advent of federal, criminal, and regulatory statutes involving business: the Sherman Antitrust Act (1890), the Internal Revenue Act (1913), and the 1934 Securities and Exchange Commission Act (SEC), to name a few. Wartime regulation of pricing and profits such as the Office of Price Administration (OPA) law and the excess-profits-tax law added further impetus to earlier laws related to mail fraud, fraud by wire, the Federal Trade Commission, the Robinson-Patman and Clayton Acts, and the Wage and Hour law. More recent federal laws that have contributed to the growth of fraud auditing include the Labor-Management Reporting and Disclosure Act, the Welfare-Pension Fund Act, Employee Retirement Income Security Act (ERISA), and the Foreign Corrupt Practices Act. These laws together with the increase in fraud in public companies, waste and abuse in government contracting, and the current public concern over white-collar crime create a greater need for further development of this new discipline.

The need for fraud-auditing talents is not related solely to compliance with new governmental regulations. Fraud-auditing skills in the private sector are also useful in most cases of financial crimes such as embezzlement, misrepresentations of financial facts, arson for profit, bankruptcy fraud, investment frauds of all manner and description, bank fraud, kickbacks and commercial bribery, computer frauds, electronic funds transfer (EFT) systems frauds, and credit card frauds; and scams and shams by vendors, suppliers, contractors, and customers.

Relatively few public accountants and internal auditors are yet trained and experienced to engage in this discipline. In the United States the largest body of trained and experienced fraud auditors comes from government audit and investigative agencies like the IRS, FBI, GAO, and the SEC. Police authorities on the state and local levels have few audit resources at their disposal and as a consequence it limits their investigation of certain white-collar crimes. The need for fraud auditing covers both public and private sectors of the economy.

2.2 WHAT SHOULD A FRAUD AUDITOR KNOW AND BE ABLE TO DO?

An effective fraud auditor should know, with some degree of depth, what fraud is from the following perspectives:

1. Human and individual
2. Organizational, cultural, and motivational
3. Economic/competitive
4. Social
5. Regulatory, legal, and evidential (how to discern, detect, and document such frauds)
6. Accounting, audit, and internal control (when, where, and how fraud is most likely to occur in books of account and in financial statements)

An effective fraud auditor should be able to do the following with some degree of competence:

1. Conduct a review of internal controls
2. Assess the strengths and weaknesses of those controls
3. Design scenarios of potential fraud losses based on identified weaknesses in internal controls
4. Identify questionable and exceptional situations with account balances

5. Identify questionable and exceptional transactions (i.e., too high, too low, too often, too rare, too much, too little, odd times, odd places, odd people)

6. Distinguish simple human errors and omissions in entries from fraudulent entries (intentional error, such as recurring small errors versus unintentional random error and ignorance)

7. Follow the flow of documents that support transactions

8. Follow the flow of funds into and out of an organization's account

9. Search for underlying support documents for questionable transactions

10. Review such documents for peculiarities such as raising of amounts; forgery; counterfeiting; fake billings; invoicing of claims; destruction of data; improper account classification; irregularities in serial sequences, quantity, pricing, extension, and footings; and substitution of copies for original documents

11. Gather and preserve evidence to corroborate asset losses, fraudulent transactions, and financial statements

12. Document and report a fraud loss for criminal, civil, or insurance-claim purposes

13. Be aware of management, administrative, and organizational policies, procedures, and practices

14. Test the organization's motivational and ethical climate

The skills of a criminal investigator are in some respects similar to those of an auditor. An auditor and a detective both seek to derive the truth, the auditor with respect to the proper accounting of business transactions and the detective/investigator with respect to the proper (legal) behavior of citizens. Both should possess inquisitive minds and challenge things that appear out of order and out of sequence, such as odd times, odd places, and odd people—in a word, things that are the *opposite* of what one would logically expect.

Laypersons call this gift investigative intuition. Investigators call it professional judgment—judgment derived from knowledge, education, training, acquired skills, and experience. No one is born with it. It is acquired, mainly in the college of hard knocks, by trial and error. It is not a formula, and it cannot actually be taught. But it can be learned.

The hunch of an amateur may not be worth much, based as it is on naiveté. The hunch of a trained investigator is worth much more, based as it is on experience, knowledge, training, and self-developed skills. So when auditors, for example, say they have discovered a fraud in accounting records by accident, it may be in fact no accident. It may not have been discovered by design or on purpose, but their trained eyes and ears have made them sensitive enough to discern the truth.

Police detectives also attribute some of their investigative insights to accident, chance, or good luck. But there again, their breakthroughs are not simply random events, but are brought about by the concentration and focus of thought on the issue at hand. It is not black magic or fortuitous circumstances.

So we would like to counter the feigned humility of some investigators and auditors by proposing that "accidental" discoveries of crimes by investigators and frauds by auditors are attributable not to pure chance but to know-how. Unfortunately not all investigators or auditors have the combined know-how. The investigative mentality comes with age, training, self-discipline, experience, and a mind-set that understands that crime and fraud are possible in any environment, at any time, by anyone, if the circumstances are ripe.

What are these circumstances? Ripe circumstances are (1) conditions in the environment, such as social values; prevailing moral and ethical standards; and economic, competitive, political, and social conditions; and (2) motives in the mental dispositions of individuals who are most likely to commit a crime.

Although the motive for a crime is not a necessary element of proof in sustaining a conviction (whereas criminal *intent* is), motivation is important to the investigator and the auditor because it tends to identify the more likely suspects when the actual culprit is unknown. The motive also helps to construct a theory of the case, that is, the who, what, when, where, how, and why of the crime. So motivation should not be discounted. It can narrow the search for the culprit and be a substantial aid in reconstructing the crime.

As a general rule, motives can be separated into four major categories: (1) psychotic, (2) economic, (3) egocentric, and (4) ideological.

Psychotic motivation can impair a successful criminal prosecution (e.g. when it calls for an insanity plea). Of the other three motivations, economic motivation is the most common. The individual wants or needs money or wealth. Egocentric motivation means the individual wants more prestige, more recognition, higher social or political status, or even a job promotion. Ideological motivation means the individual feels that his cause or values are morally superior to those of the victim, or he or she feels exploited, abused, or discriminated against by the victim.

Motives should be looked at from another perspective as well; for example, a series of emotions may also serve as motives (e.g., motives such as jealousy; spite; revenge; anger; greed; bigotry; hatred; pride; covetousness; gluttony; and sloth; or fears of ridicule, rejection, poverty, sickness, pain or death, failure, loss, and even fear of uncertainty).

It is clear that what a competent investigator must know best is people and their motivations—their needs, wants, demands, and desires; their values, beliefs, and attitudes; and their individual peculiarities.

Auditors, if they hope to become fraud auditors, must have a similar inclination toward the study of people. They must also know how to identify and locate culprits and witnesses and how to interview them as well as how to gather, classify, and preserve information and evidence and how to assess its value, weight, and significance.

2.3 THIRTEEN PRINCIPLES OF FRAUD AUDITING

1. Fraud auditing is unlike financial auditing. It is more a mind-set than a methodology.

2. Fraud auditors are unlike financial auditors. Fraud auditors focus on exceptions, oddities, accounting irregularities, and patterns of conduct, not on errors and omissions.

3. Fraud auditing is primarily learned from experience, not from audit textbooks or last year's work papers. Learning to be a fraud auditor means learning to think like a thief (i.e., "Where are the weakest links in this chain of internal controls?").

4. From an audit perspective, fraud is an intentional misrepresentation of financial facts of a material nature. From a fraud-audit perspective, fraud is an intentional misrepresentation of financial facts.

5. Frauds are committed for economic, egocentric, ideological, and psychotic reasons. Of the four, the economic motive is the most common.

6. Fraud tends to encompass a theory structured around motive, opportunity and benefit.

7. Fraud in a computerized accounting environment can be committed at any state of processing, (i.e., input, throughput, or output). Input frauds (i.e., entering false and fraudulent data) are the most common.

8. The most common fraudulent schemes by lower-level employees involve disbursements (i.e., payables, payroll, and benefit and expense claims).

9. The most common fraudulent schemes by higher-level managers involve "profit smoothing" (i.e., deferring expenses, booking sales too early, overstating inventory).

10. Accounting-type frauds are caused more often by absence of controls than by loose controls.

11. Fraud incidents are not growing exponentially, but fraud losses are.

12. Accounting frauds are discovered more often by accident than by financial audit purposes or design. Over 90 percent of financial frauds are discovered by accident.

13. Fraud prevention is a matter of adequate controls and a work environment in which a high value is placed on personal honesty and fair dealing.

2.4 FINANCIAL AUDITING VERSUS FRAUD AUDITING

Financial auditing is intended to uncover material deviations and variances from standards of acceptable accounting and auditing practice. But when pretense is used to disguise a transaction or to cover it up, the financial auditor is not likely to become suspicious. Furthermore, the assumption of management integrity creates at times a false sense of security for the financial auditor over the legitimacy of financial transactions. Looking *behind* and *beyond* the transaction forces the fraud auditor to ignore assumptions and to focus on substance instead. The questions the fraud auditor has uppermost in mind are not how the accounting system and internal controls stack up against AICPA and CICA standards but:

1. Where are the weakest links in this system's chain of controls?

2. What deviations from conventional good accounting practices are possible in this system?

3. How are off-line transactions handled, and who can authorize such transactions?

4. What would be the simplest way to compromise this system?

5. What control features in this system can be bypassed by higher authorities?

6. What is the nature of the work environment?

Auditing for fraud is therefore more of an intuitive process than it is a formal, analytic methodology. It is more of an art form than it is a science. As a consequence it is difficult to teach. Skill depends on the right mind-set (thinking like a thief, probing for weaknesses) and practice. But it is not technique one should master; it is mental disposition (i.e., doggedness and persistence). No lead, no shred of evidence is ever too small to have relevance. One seeks relevant information, organizes it in some meaningful way, and then sees what pattern it creates.

The patterns to look for are the exceptions and oddities, the things that do not fit in an organized scheme because they seem too large, too small, too frequent, too rare, too high, too low, too ordinary, too extraordinary, too many, or too few, or feature odd times, odd places, odd hours, odd people, and odd combinations. In a word, one looks for the unusual rather than the usual. Then one goes behind and beyond those transactions to reconstruct what may have led to them and what followed. A more complete assessment of fraud is possible if the data that precedes or follows a questionable transaction are available.

From an accounting and audit standpoint fraud is an intentional misrepresentation of a material fact in the books of account and ultimately the financial statements. The misrepresentation may be directed against organizational outsiders like shareholders or creditors or against the organization itself by way of covering up or disguising embezzlement, incompetence, misapplications of funds, and theft, or improper use of organizational assets by officers, employees, and agents.

Fraud may also be directed against an organization by outsiders, (vendors, suppliers, contractors, consultants, and customers) by way of overbilling, double billing, substitution of inferior materials, or misrepresentations as to quality and value of goods purchased or the credit standing of customers. Such outsiders may also be guilty of corrupting insiders (commercial bribery).

Fraud, theft, embezzlement, and commercial bribery are the paramount concerns of fraud auditors. Fraud auditing is the discipline used to discourage, discern, and document such incidents. These incidents may occur over a period of years before they are discovered. Auditing for fraud means identifying intentional irregularities in accounting practices, procedures, and controls.

Financial auditing, as distinguished from fraud auditing, concentrates on the present—on the adequacy of internal controls, on the reliability, validity, and mathematical accuracy of today's entries. But such a narrow focus does not provide a historical perspective. Reasonableness tests, when not related to past relationships and trends, do not provide enough insight. For that reason we say fraud auditing looks beyond, behind, and before current transactions. Fraud auditing occupies itself as much with the past as the present.

Frauds of this kind occur most often when the following conditions exist:

1. Internal controls are absent, weak, or loosely enforced.
2. Employees are hired without due consideration for their honesty and integrity.
3. Employees are poorly managed, exploited, abused, or placed under great stress to accomplish financial goals and objectives.
4. Management models are themselves corrupt, inefficient, or incompetent.
5. A trusted employee has an unresolvable personal problem, usually of a financial nature, brought on by family medical needs, or alcoholism, drug abuse, excessive gambling, or expensive tastes.
6. The industry of which the company is a part has a history or tradition of corruption.
7. The company has fallen on bad times (i.e., is losing money or market share, or its products or services are becoming passé).

Physical custody of property, access to accounting records, and knowledge and authority to override controls are the main ingredients of fraud in books of account and in financial statements.

People who have access to corporate assets and knowledge of the internal and accounting controls, or who hold management roles of the sort where they can exercise an override of such controls, are in the best position to commit financial frauds against their companies. The threat of fraud is greatest at senior management levels because access to assets and authority to bypass controls is greatest at that level. But financial fraud is also possible among those personnel with accounting, finance, data processing, and property-handling responsibilities. They too may have access to accounting records and can use that knowledge and authority to compromise controls and access corporate assets.

There is no simple recipe for conducting a fraud audit, nor are there any generally accepted checklists or patterned interviews. Fraud is a human phenomenon. Humans vary a great deal, as do frauds, in terms of the techniques used.

Most frauds, embezzlements, and thefts of corporate assets are not discovered in the course of routine financial audits. Knowledge of their existence usually comes to light on the basis of (1) an allegation, complaint, or a rumor of fraud by a third party (a disgruntled supplier or a fellow employee), (2) an investigator's intuition or general suspicion that something is awry, (3) an exception from expectation made by a person senior to the suspect (an unacceptable condition, profits, sales, costs, assets, or liabilities are too low or too high), or (4) the sudden discovery that something is missing—cash, property, reports, files, documents, or data. But rarely does an auditor know at the outset that a fraud, theft, or embezzlement was in fact committed. At the outset, one has some rather sketchy information at best and applies the investigative mentality: How to determine whether a fraud, theft, or embezzlement has in fact occurred? Here is an example of a fraud auditor's thought process. The objective is to determine whether a crime exists. A crime exists when there exist the following: a proven loss of something of value to a victim, a perpetrator who caused that loss, and a law that makes that loss a crime. So the immediate facts to determine are whether there exists (1) a criminal law, (2) an apparent breach of that law, (3) a perpetrator, and (4) a victim. These are some of the steps in the fraud auditor's thinking:

1. Acquire all available corporate documents relating to the allegation.
2. Meet with the individual making the allegation to determine if the allegation makes sense and assess the degree of emotion expressed.
3. Assess the allegation against the available documentation in order to determine the next appropriate move.
4. Determine, if necessary, whether further documentation is available from the company. If so, where? Should other people within the company be interviewed?
5. Assess the corporate environment relative to the person in question.
6. Ask, can a theory of fraud be developed at this stage? That is, is there motive and opportunity that could possibly benefit the person?

7. Ask, does the available evidence make sense? Does it meet the test of business reality?

8. Should third parties outside the company be interviewed? Do I have a right to meet with these people and examine their documents?

9. Are the proper people within the company informed of the current situation and its direction?

10. How far back in time should one go?

11. Was the problem there before the person assumed a new position?

12. Was the problem present at the person's previous position?

13. What public documents are available?

Accounting-type frauds are usually accompanied by the modification, alteration, destruction, or counterfeiting of accounting information. But accounting information either can be intentionally or accidentally modified, altered, and destroyed, as by human error or omission. The first objective for the fraud auditor then is to determine whether a discrepancy in accounting records can be attributable to human error. If so, there may be no actual fraud. If the discrepancy (missing records, destroyed records, modified records, counterfeit records, errors, omissions) cannot be attributable to accident or human error, then a full-scale fraud audit/investigation should follow.

Evidence gathered may consist of the testimony of witnesses, confessions of perpetrators, documents, items (means and instruments, or fruits of the crime), and perhaps the testimony of experts. One of those experts may have to be a forensic accountant or fraud auditor, someone who can explain in layperson's terms, the financial information available modified or destroyed records, data, documents, and files.

Auditors are most likely to uncover in the course of routine financial audits cases of active or ongoing embezzlement, *if* they have some degree of fraud awareness. Otherwise the probability of discovering embezzlement is about 10 percent, if you can believe auditors impressions. (Auditors claim 90 percent of the frauds they uncover are found by accident.)

2.5 THINKING AS A FRAUD AUDITOR

Fraud auditors and detectives tend to be primarily "thinker" types. They are thinkers in the sense that they deal with situations requiring objectivity on their part. Personal feelings and personal biases are not appropriate for making sound decisions and drawing logical conclusions and inferences.

Fraud auditors and detectives tend also to be intuitive in the sense that they enjoy solving new and different problems given a minimum amount of information. Continuous financial auditing would not be the fraud auditor's normal cup of tea.

Fraud auditors, in circumstances in which evidence is sparse or destroyed and sometimes even nonexistent, can theorize about the facts and play on hunches. They are sensitive to nonverbal cues, are spontaneous in solving such problems, and can refine and rework a problem with a variety of approaches until the problem is solved. They rely more on ingenuity in their work than on a canned audit program.

We owe decisional classifications (sensers, intuitors, thinkers, and feelers) to Carl Jung, who proposed the taxonomy some 60 years ago. Jung also suggested that each of us tends to be dominant in only one of the four functions, but this dominant function is backed up by a paired opposite. So the four basic decision combinations are (1) sensation/thinking, (2) intuition/thinking, (3) sensation/feeling, and (4) intuition/feeling.

Updating Jung's theory with recent neurological research, we can also say that some people are left-brain dominant (rational, analytical, sequential, logical, systematic), and some people are right-brain dominant (creative, emotional, intuitive, holistic). (See Exhibit 2.1)

Left Hemisphere--------------------Right Hemisphere

Sensation/ Thinking Financial Auditor	Intuition/ Thinking Fraud Auditor		Sensation/ Feeling Teacher	Intuition/ Feeling Artist

EXHIBIT 2.1

There is another distinction between financial auditing and fraud auditing. Financial auditing tends to look at events, transactions, and environments in terms of their overt aspects, whereas fraud auditors tend to look at events, transactions, and environments in terms of their covert aspects. (See Exhibit 2.2)

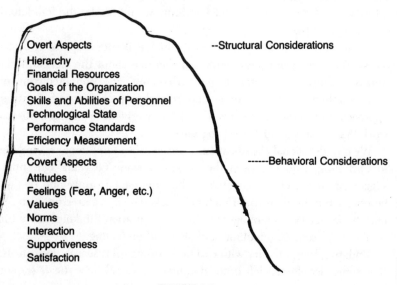

Overt Aspects   --Structural Considerations
Hierarchy
Financial Resources
Goals of the Organization
Skills and Abilities of Personnel
Technological State
Performance Standards
Efficiency Measurement

Covert Aspects   ------Behavioral Considerations
Attitudes
Feelings (Fear, Anger, etc.)
Values
Norms
Interaction
Supportiveness
Satisfaction

EXHIBIT 2.2

Everything we see above the surface is important, but there is a great deal under the surface that also merits close attention. So it appears that financial auditors tend to focus on the structural aspects of control. Are they there, in place, in adequate quantity, and being monitored? Fraud auditors tend to preoccupy themselves with the behavioral aspects of control. Can they be breached? If so, by whom? Under what conditions or circumstances?

Intuition, which we define as professional judgment, is a quality and disposition of the mind. It comes mainly from personal experience. Education and training play some part in its development, but education and training cannot do it all. It is difficult to write a how-to book on fraud auditing; how-to books present their contents in the form of cookbook recipes, but fraud involves so many variables in terms of fraud types, defrauder types, victim types, crime methods, techniques, tools, means, and instruments, that any effort to unify them into some comprehensive theory of causation or solution seems impossible. So it is more difficult to train fraud auditors in a methodical way. On-the-job training is perhaps the best instructional method; one must experience fraud to know it best. But the experience can be borrowed from others—it does not have to be based totally on personal experience. The study of cases, especially those that have been subjects of books, is of particular value.

The knack of intuition can be acquired if you retain an open, objective, and inquisitive mind—not necessarily an analytical mind so much as a mind that can synthesize data, to put it all together in some sort of scenario of what possibly happened. The process is like doing jigsaw puzzles. They can be put together quicker after you develop a knack.

Mystery stories are generally exercises in deductive logic, and most laypersons believe crimes can be detected and proven that way. Some can be. But crime and fraud discernment generally involve the application of inductive as well as deductive logic. An instructive recurring theme in most mystery stories is the solution of crimes through a brilliant flash of insight at some point in the investigation. Some minor or oddball thing happened or was found or observed that ultimately led to the crime's solution. Literary critics call this flash of insight "the deduction of staggering conclusions from trifling indications." A minor fact became the major fact in unraveling the crime or identifying the killer. It is not our habit to disagree with literary critics, but we do not believe that their language is correct. The process they call deduction is more like synthesis. It was not a missing piece in a jigsaw puzzle that solved the crime, but a missing link in the chain of evidence that brought the insight to the fore. It can be described as seeing the *whole* and the *hole* all at once. It is the union of time, space, and energy that causes the flash. That is intuition. But this knack for seeing the hole and the whole all at once does not come without experience and the right mind-set. Mind-set means a predisposition to believe in the things you see, feel, taste, touch, smell, and experience—to believe in your own competence. Some people call the latter "arrogance," but it is not that at all. Good investigators do not necessarily have a sixth sense. They are just open to their senses, open to suggestion, open to oddities. They can see both the doughnut and the hole. Sherlock Holmes had this talent for seeing the oddity, the dog that did not bark.

In summary, the most accepted scientific methods for deriving truth involve the use of deductive and inductive reasoning. In deductive reasoning one proceeds from the general to the specific, whereas in inductive reasoning one proceeds from the specific to the general. Inductive reasoning involves an empirical approach to truth, that is, one takes a representative sample of the whole and predicts a probable outcome based on that sample. In deductive reasoning one makes clinical observations, physical examinations, and interrogations, and eliminates the extraneous, then draws inferences to arrive at certain generalizations or conclusions. Financial auditors tend to utilize the inductive approach, whereas investigators tend to utilize the deductive approach. Fraud auditors may have to utilize both approaches in developing their investigative mentality.

REFERENCES

1. *American Jurisprudence*, 2d ed., Vol. 1, Sec. 15, Rochester, N.Y.: The Lawyers Cooperative Publishing Co., 1962, pp. 365–366.
2. *Statement on Internal Auditing Standards*, Institute of Internal Auditors, 1984.
3. "Generally Accepted Accounting Standards,"*AICPA Professional Standards*, Vol. 1, AV Sec. 327, New York: American Institute of Certified Public Accountants, pp. 322–323.
4. U.S. v. Arthur Young & Co., March 21. 1984.
5. *In Our Opinion*, July 1985.
6. Financial Fraud Detection and Disclosure Act, H.R. Doc. No. 4886, 99th Cong. 2d Sess.
7. Wilfred C. Uecker, Arthur P. Brief, and William R. Kinney, Jr., "Perception of the Internal and External Auditor as a Deterrent to Corporate Irregularities," *The Accounting Review*, (July 1981), pp. 465–478.
8. John Shad, Chairman of Securities and Exchange Commission, testimony before House Subcommittee on Oversight and Investigations.

3

PREVENTION AND DETECTION AWARENESS FOR THE FRAUD AUDITOR

Preventing fraud is what this book is all about. Our primary goal is to reduce incidents of accounting-type frauds. Our secondary goal is to reduce the amount of the losses attributable to such frauds. With those goals in mind, we offer the following "invitations to fraud" for whatever instructive value that list contains.

3.1 INVITATIONS TO CORPORATE FRAUD, THEFT, AND EMBEZZLEMENT

1. Make profit the only corporate objective and the only criterion for performance appraisal.
2. Create a corporate culture in which everyone knows the cost of everything but not the value of integrity.
3. Create a corporate culture in which profit and economic incentives are the only motivators.
4. Fail to establish and to communicate an effective code for corporate conduct.
5. Create strong and authoritarian management controls but do not monitor them for compliance.
6. Ignore complaints from customers, stockholders, or employees.

7. Fail to monitor management override of internal controls.

8. Make internal communication a one-way process—top down.

9. Fail to enforce or monitor non-arm's-length transactions.

10. Ignore the importance of effective personnel policies.

11. Assume competitors are less than ethical in order to rationalize a competitive behavior as fair and justified.

3.2 LANDMARK CASES IN CORPORATE FRAUD

What factors in an organization's internal environment lead to fraudulent behavior by executives, middle managers, and lower-level employees? Let us examine the following cases as examples:

1. *SEC v. McCormick & Co.*, Civil Action No. 82-3614 (D.D.C. 1982)

2. *SEC v. AM International, Inc.*, Civil Action No. 83-1526, (D.D.C. May 2, 1983), Litigation Release No. 9980, (February 27, 1984)

3. *SEC v. U.S. Surgical Corp.*, Civil Action No. 84-0589, (D.D.C. 1984), Litigation Release No. 10293, (February 27, 1984)

In the *McCormick* case, the Commission's complaint alleged that McCormick inflated reported current earnings by deferring recognition of various expenses and by increasing reported revenues by accounting for goods ready for shipment as current sales, even though they were not shipped until a later period. These irregularities occurred in autonomous divisions and involved a number of employees in middle-management roles. These employees believed the improper practices were the only way to achieve the profit goals set arbitrarily by a distant, centralized corporate management. Several employees stated they viewed their activities as a team effort, all for the benefit of the company. There was no evidence that corporate funds were diverted for the personal benefit of any McCormick employee.

In *AM International*, the Commission alleged that AMI grossly overstated its results of operations, assets, and shareholders' equity, understated liabilities, and misstated statements of changes in financial position.

How did AMI accomplish this? Inventory losses were deferred and ending inventory overstated; books were kept open after cutoff dates to increase reported sales and earnings; sales were recorded although products were not shipped; sales were inflated by deliberate double-billing; operating leases were recorded as sales; allowances for losses were arbitrarily reduced without any basis whatsoever; sales were recorded although the products were shipped only to branch offices and a public warehouse, not to customers; accounting policies were changed to increase earnings without disclosure of the changes in policy; known errors that caused increased earnings were ignored; intercompany accounts were out of balance and the differences arbitrarily reclassified as inventories; known inaccuracies in books and records were not investigated, let alone resolved; costs of sales were manipulated; and accounts payable were simply not recorded.

The organizational environment aired in the AMI complaint made a highly negative impression on the Commission. Two excerpts from the SEC complaint exemplify this environment:[1]

> During the course of the 1980 fiscal year AM International's financial position deteriorated and its management then applied increasing pressure on the divisions to meet performance goals. Such pressure consisted of, among other means, threatened dismissals, actual dismissals, and character attacks on certain of the division's senior management. This pressure was in turn applied by the division's senior management to middle management. These pressures were motivated in part by the desire of AMI to have a public offering of its securities in the fall of 1980, and the belief that a pretax profit of $10 to $12 million for the 1980 fiscal year necessary in order to proceed with the offering. . . .

> In response to the pressure. . .various divisions. . .engaged in widespread and pervasive accounting irregularities. . .in order to present results of operations which conformed to budget performance objectives. Throughout the 1980 fiscal year AMI's corporate headquarters learned of many instances of accounting irregularities employed by its divisions. Despite this knowledge, AMI continued to pressure its divisions to meet projected operating results.

The Commission's complaint in *U.S. Surgical* alleged that Surgical:

1. Issued falsified purchase orders to vendors who, in turn, submitted untrue invoices so that Surgical's reported cost of parts was decreased and its reported costs of materials was improperly capitalized by over $4 million

2. Shipped significant quantities of unordered products to customers and recorded them as sales

3. Improperly treated shipments on consignments to its dealers, salespeople, and certain foreign entities as sales, resulting in a cumulative overstatement of income by over $2 million

4. Improperly failed to write off assets that could not be located or had been scrapped, and capitalized certain operating costs as overhead, increasing earnings by millions of dollars

5. Improperly capitalized approximately $4 million of legal costs, purportedly for the defense of certain patents, when those costs did not relate to the defense of patents but were recurring operating expenses

3.3 HIGH-FRAUD/LOW-FRAUD ENVIRONMENTS

Employee fraud, theft, and embezzlement is more prevalent in some organizations than in others. Conventional wisdom among members of the audit and security communities would suggest that the organizations that are most vulnerable are the ones with the weakest management, accounting, and security controls, and they therefore propose as solutions:

1. Tight accounting and audit controls

2. Thorough screening of applicants for employment

3. Close supervision and monitoring of employee performance and behavior

4. Explicit rules against theft, fraud, embezzlement, sabotage, and information piracy, and strict sanctions for their breach

Although we would not disagree with those solutions, we do believe other considerations exist that also have an impact on employee crime. Organizations that are most vulnerable to employee skullduggery can also be distinguished from those that are less vulnerable by the environmental and cultural contrasts shown in Table 3.1.

TABLE 3.1
The Corporate Fraud Environment

Potential for Fraud	
High Fraud Potential	Low Fraud Potential
Management Style	Management Style
Autocratic	Participative
Management Orientation	Management Orientation
Low trust	High trust
X Theory	Y Theory
Power driven	Achievement driven
Distribution of Authority	Distribution of Authority
Centralized, reserved by	Decentralized, delegated to
top management	all levels
Planning	Planning
Centralized	Decentralized
Short range	Long range
Performance	Performance
Measured quantitatively and	Measured both qualitatively and
on a short-term basis	quantitatively and on a long-term basis
Profit Focused	Customer Focused
Management by Crisis	Management by Objectives
Reporting by Routine	Reporting by Exception
Rigid Rules Strongly Policed	Reasonable Rules Fairly Enforced
Primary Management Concerns	Primary Management Concerns
Preservation of capital	Profit optimization
Profit maximization	Human, then capital and technological asset utilization
Reward System	Reward System
Punitive	Reinforcing
Penurious	Generous
Politically administered	Fairly administered
Feedback on Performance	Feedback on Performance
Critical	Positive
Negative	Supportive
Interaction Mode	Interaction Mode
Issues and personal differences	Issues and personal differences
are skirted or repressed	are confronted and addressed openly
Payoffs for Good Behavior	Payoffs for Good Behavior
Mainly monetary	Recognition, promotion, added responsibility, choice assignments, plus money

(continued)

TABLE 3.1 (Continued)
The Corporate Fraud Environment

Potential for Fraud	
High Fraud Potential	Low Fraud Potential

Business Ethics
  Ambivalent, rides the tides
	Business Ethics
	  Clearly defined and regularly
	    followed

Internal Relationships
  Highly competitive, hostile
	Internal Relationships
	  Friendly, competitive,
	    supportive

Values and Beliefs
  Economic, political,
    self-centered
	Values and Beliefs
	  Social, spiritual, group-centered

Success Formula
  Works harder
	Success Formula
	  Works smarter

Biggest Human Resource Problems
  High turnover
  Burnout
  Grievances
  Absenteeism
	Biggest Human Resource Problem
	  Not enough promotional
	    opportunities for all the talent

Company Loyalty
  Low
	Company Loyalty
	  High

Major Financial Concern
  Cash flow shortage
	Major Financial Concern
	  Opportunities for new
	    investments

Growth Pattern
  Sporadic
	Growth Pattern
	  Consistent

Relationships with Competitors
  Hostile
	Relationship with Competitors
	  Professional

Innovativeness
  Copycat, reactive
	Innovativeness
	  Leader, proactive

CEO Characteristics
  Swinger, braggart,
    self-interested, driver,
    insensitive to people,
    feared, insecure, gambler,
    impulsive, tight-fisted,
    number- and things-oriented,
    profit seeker, vain,
    bombastic, highly emotional,
    partial, pretends to be more
    than he is
	CEO Characteristics
	  Professional, decisive,
	    fast-paced, friendly,
	    respected by peers, secure,
	    risk taker, thoughtful,
	    generous with personal time
	    and money, products- and
	    markets-oriented, builder,
	    helper, self-confident,
	    composed, calm, deliberate,
	    even disposition, fair, knows
	    who he is, what he is, and
	    where he is

TABLE 3.1 *(Continued)*
The Corporate Fraud Environment

Potential for Fraud	
High Fraud Potential	Low Fraud Potential
Management Structure, Systems and Controls	Management Structure, Systems and Controls
Bureaucratic	Collegial
Regimented	Systematic
Inflexible	Open to change
Imposed controls	Self-controlled
Many-tiered structure, vertical	Flat structure, horizontal
Everything documented, a rule for everything	Documentation adequate but not burdensome; some discretion afforded
Internal Communication	Internal Communication
Formal, written, stiff, pompous, ambiguous, CYA	Informal, oral, clear, friendly, open, candid
Peer Relationships	Peer Relationships
Hostile, aggressive, rivalrous	Cooperative, friendly, trusting

Source: Jack Bologna, in *Forensic Accounting Review*, 1985.

3.3.1 Other Environmental Red Flags

1. Do employees have an economic reason to cheat?

   Are salaries and fringe benefits equitable and competitive with other similar firms in the same market?

   Are pressures for production and profitable performance so great that people are burning out or becoming disgruntled?

   Are employee evaluations and salary reviews based on fair and objective criteria?

   Are promotions based on merit and contribution and administered fairly, impartially, and openly?

   Are job-related goals and objectives imposed on subordinates rather than negotiated with them?

2. Does the company suffer from a "we−they" syndrome: Management versus nonmanagement personnel or middle management versus top management?

3. Do conflicts abound among the top-management group over issues that involve corporate philosophy, purpose, direction, or ethics?

4. Is there evidence of spite, hate, hostility, or jealousy among the firm's top-management group?

5. Do employees feel oppressed, abused, exploited, or neglected by top management?

6. What is the company's past history with respect to:

   Labor-management relations?

   Turnover of top executives?

   Moonlighting and conflict of interest by employees and executives?

   Vandalism, theft, and sabotage by employees?

   Corruption of customers?

   Corruption by vendors or competitors?

   Corruption of labor leaders, regulatory authorities, and political officials?

   Association of executives with organized-crime figures?

   High living by executives?

   Lack of concern for truth in advertising or marketing its products or services?

   Convictions for business-related crimes?

7. What is the history of the firm and the industry regarding regulatory compliance?

8. What is past, current, and future profitability of the firm?

9. Are there litigation and complaints pending against the firm by regulatory authorities, vendors, customers, creditors, and competitors?

3.4 HOW CAN MANAGEMENT AND CORPORATE FRAUD BE DETECTED?

Detecting fraud is a matter of acknowledging:

1. That fraud exists

2. That any organization can become either a victim of fraud or a perpetrator of fraud

3. That certain weaknesses in internal controls and human character can be conducive to fraud
4. That certain tests of internal controls and tests of the organization's motivational environment can provide some insight on the possibility of fraud in that environment
5. That the key to fraud auditing is training the mind to see both the doughnut and the hole

The hole we speak of consists of errors and irregularities, but of the type that seem to be a little more than just within the normal bounds of human error and inconsistency. Perhaps "oddity" would be a better word to describe the anomalies one looks for in fraud auditing.

An oddity is something different than expected as to time, place, personality, or amount. The difference does not necessarily have to be large. An accumulation of small differences is often the very essence of a sophisticated large fraud (i.e., the "salami-slicing" technique in computer fraud, in which a programmer instructs the computer to shave a dime or dollar from everyone's paycheck and add the total amount to his own paycheck).

Small differences are what the fraud auditor concentrates on, whereas financial auditing is designed and intended to detect large differences. We call those differences substantial, as though an exponential accumulation of small differences were insubstantial. In this sense fraud auditing is distinguished from financial auditing: financial auditing focuses on large differences. The road to scientific insight has always been paved with small exceptions and irregularities. In essence we might say that fraud auditing deals more with exceptions than general rules.

Here, then, are a few exceptions fraud auditors should look for:

1. Transactions that are odd as to:
   Time (of day, week, month, year, or season)
   Frequency (too many, too few)
   Places (too far, too near, and too "far out")
   Amount (too high, too low, too consistent, too alike, too different)
   Parties or personalities ("related" parties, "oddball" personalities, strange and estranged relationships between parties, management performing clerical functions)

2. Internal controls that are unenforced or too often compromised by higher authorities

3. Employee motivation, morale, and job satisfaction levels that are chronically low

4. A corporate culture and reward system that supports unethical behavior toward employees, customers, competitors, lenders, and shareholders

Fraud abounds in environments in which there is low regard for truth, justice, and fair dealing and high regard for monetary rewards and personal vanity.

3.5 TELLTALE SIGNS OF MANAGEMENT AND CORPORATE FRAUD

In every case of management and corporate fraud there are telltale signs of the fraud in existence for some period of time before the fraud itself is detected or disclosed by a third party. These signs may be as follows:

1. Significant observed changes from the past behavior pattern of the defrauder

2. Knowledge that the defrauder was undergoing emotional trauma in his or her home life or work life

3. Knowledge that the defrauder was betting heavily, drinking heavily, had a very expensive social life, or was sexually promiscuous

4. Knowledge that the defrauder was heavily in debt

5. Audit findings deemed to be errors and irregularities that were considered immaterial at the time

6. Knowledge that the company was having financial difficulties such as frequent cash flow shortages, declining sales and/or net profits, and loss of market share

7. Knowledge that management was showing increasing signs of incompetence (i.e., poor planning, organization, communication, controls, motivation, and delegation; management indecision and confusion about corporate mission, goals, and strategies; and management ignorance of conditions in the industry and in the general economy)

8. Substantial growth beyond the industry norm in regulated industries

These precipitating or predisposing conditions and events are called in crisis-management parlance *prodromal* or warning signs. (The word, derived from the Greek for "running before," means "running in a precrisis mode.")

For example, when a major midwestern bank came close to failure a few years ago, there were some prodromal conditions extant before the bank had to be bailed out by the Federal Deposit Insurance Corporation (FDIC). One such event was the discovery by the bank's internal auditors that a bank officer who had purchased $800 million in oil and gas loans from the Penn Square Bank had been the recipient of $565,000 in loans from Penn Square Bank. Was that a red flag, a prodromal event? It is alleged that the bank's top management was not overly concerned about that kind of evidence of impropriety. It issued only a reprimand, a mild rebuke, because the officer also brought in a portfolio of loans that could earn a gross return rate of 20 percent—if the loans performed. Unfortunately, most of the loans had to be written off a short time later.

As can be seen, not dealing with indications of management fraud when they first surface does not end it. And not dealing with it promptly when indications do fully surface may be quite costly in terms of the cash loss and loss of corporate image. Indications that first appear as oddities, for example, should be assessed as a possible fraud. One may be able to insure against the cash loss itself but the damage to the image of the company and its products and services may be irreparable, particularly if the company is in the financial services business where faith, confidence, and trust in the industry and institution are the critical factors of success.

One further bit of advice: Prodromal events can become a way out for a company's fidelity insurance underwriter. The company auditor may be accused of acquiescing by ignoring an indicator of fraud and not reporting the fraud within the time specified in the policy. If the insurance company's position holds up in court, an employer may not be able to recover on the cash loss. If so, the corporation's image may be damaged even further—the stockholders may decide to sue for managerial negligence.

3.5.1 Badges of Top-Management Fraud

A review of behaviors of corporate defrauders leads one to suggest the following profile for top-management defrauders:

1. They tend to have highly material personal values. Success to them means financial success, not professional recognition.

2. They tend to treat people as objects, not individuals, and often as objects for exploitation.

3. They are highly self-centered.

4. They are often eccentric in the way they display their wealth or spend their money. They tend to be conspicuous consumers and often boast of things they have acquired, the friends they have in high office, and all the fine places they have visited.

5. They boast about their cunning achievements and winnings more than their losses.

6. They appear to be reckless or careless with facts and often enlarge on them.

7. They appear to be hard working, almost compulsive, but most of their time at work is spent in scheming and designing short cuts to get ahead or beat the competition.

8. They may gamble or drink a great deal.

9. They buy expensive gifts for their families, usually to compensate for spending so little time with them.

10. They show great hostility toward people who oppose their views. They feel exempt from accountability and controls because of their station or position.

11. They create a great deal of turnover among their subordinates and often set off one subordinate against another.

12. They play favorites among their subordinates, but the relationship can cool very quickly because a subordinate often falls from grace after one mistake, even an insignificant mistake.

13. They more often manage by crisis than by objectives. They tend to drift with the times and have no long-range plans.

14. They tend to override internal controls with impunity and argue forcefully for less formality in controls.

15. They demand absolute loyalty from subordinates but they themselves are loyal only to their own self-interests.

16. They have few real friends within their own industry or company. Their competitors and colleagues often dislike them.

3.5.2 Badges of Lower-Level Fraud

The above behavior descriptors are symptomatic of top-management fraud. What about lower-level profit-center managers—are there any patterns of behavior at those levels? Yes. First, recall that subordinates tend to mimic the behaviors of their superiors. So the preceding listing of fraud badges is useful here, too. But lower-level defrauders have symptoms of their own as well. Here are some of the conditions found in their environment:

1. Great pressure is exerted by their superiors to achieve high performance—higher sales, lower costs, more profits. No justification or excuse is tolerated by top management for less than expected or demanded sales, cost, and profit targets.

2. Bonuses are tied to short-term performance levels and do not take economic or competitive realities into consideration.

3. Internal controls are absent or loosely enforced.

4. Management controls consist mainly of pressures for performance: "Make your numbers come out right or we'll get somebody else."

5. Business ethics are subordinated to economic self-interests.

6. Vendors and suppliers are squeezed for the last ounce of profitability in their goods, wares, and services.

7. There is a great deal of confusion about duties and responsibilities among subordinates.

8. A high level of hostility exists among subordinates and between lower-level managers and their line and staff superiors.

9. They believe the present level of responsibility exceeds the original job description.

3.6 EMBEZZLEMENT: WOULD YOU KNOW ONE IF YOU SAW ONE?

Detection of embezzlement is possible (1) through the traditional control concepts of separation of duties and audit trails, (2) through periodic financial and operational audits, (3) through the gathering of intelligence on the lifestyles and personal habits of employees, (4) through allegations and complaints of fellow employees, (5) through the logging of exceptions to prescribed controls and procedures, (6) through the review of variances in operating performance expectations (standards, goals, objectives, budgets, and plans), (7) through the intuition of the embezzler's superiors, and (8) through generalized suspicion (neurotic paranoia).

As can be seen from the above list of embezzlement-detection techniques, some are proactive approaches and others are reactive. Proactive approaches include (1) adequate internal controls, (2) financial and operational audits, (3) intelligence gathering, (4) logging of exceptions, and (5) review of variances. Reactive approaches include (1) allegations and complaints, (2) intuition, and (3) suspicion. All have a place in the general framework of embezzlement prevention, but ideally we should focus more on the proactive approaches than the reactive, although at the moment it would seem the reactive approaches are more commonly used.

Are there any other audit and investigative caveats to embezzlements? Yes, there are several others: First, embezzlers usually do not make one grand hit for a million dollars and then run away. They are not hit-and-run criminals like confidence men and women are. Their peculations very often go on for years and very often get larger and larger over time. Sometimes this increase is necessary to maintain the scheme.

Second, each embezzler has a pattern of theft that is somewhat unique but discernable to an experienced fraud auditor (e.g., an account category that gets an inordinate amount of padding to cover up the loss; a particular step in the audit-trail procedures that often gets bypassed or overridden; a favorite customer supplier or contractor whose account balance gets manipulated; or an input document that often is fabricated, counterfeited, or forged). Most long-term embezzlement schemes, after discovery, are found to be very simple. This is a reflection of the embezzler's knowledge of the accounting system and those who interface with it. Fraudulent-pattern recognition is the unique skill of a trained and experienced fraud auditor.

3.7 IS CORPORATE FRAUD CYCLICAL?

Every aspect of economic life seems to have a season, a cycle, or a wave. These variations in movement over time facilitate business planning and government economic policy. Although the highs and lows of such economic trends cannot be predicted with precision on a short-term basis, they can be predicted from a long-term perspective. For example, the general economy of any country (and perhaps the world) goes from periods of prosperity to crisis to liquidation to expansion to upswing and finally back to prosperity.

Does the economic cycle have any impact on the incidence of corporate fraud? Logic would dictate that it does. Corporate fraud, being mainly a manifestation of economic greed and need, may well follow a similar cycle. But does fraudulent conduct by corporate executives peak out during good economic times or during bad times? The answer is during both good and bad times.

Fraudulent conduct by corporate managers peaks at the top of an economic cycle when it is greed based and at the bottom of the economic cycle when it is need based.

3.8 CAN MANAGEMENT CONTROLS BECOME TOO MUCH OF A GOOD THING?

Establishing effective and efficient management controls tends to be a matter of balancing costs against benefits. Tipping the balance to either extreme of overcontrol or undercontrol is inefficient and ineffective. But the cost of implementing controls is far easier to calculate than the intended benefits of such controls because costs tend to be quantitative whereas benefits tend to be qualitative.

Deciding how much control should be exercised in any organization is not a simple matter. Furthermore, both economic considerations and behavior considerations have to be weighed. Economic considerations include direct and consequential costs (acquisition, implementation, and maintenance costs). Behavioral considerations have to do with the impact that controls may have on personal productivity. Do controls add to one's work burdens, impose additional or distasteful tasks, make one less efficient, more suspicious of others, less trusting, or less trusted? Do control costs have an impact on human performance and job satisfaction? Worse yet, do controls take on the form of absolute rules, prohibitions, and mandatory actions and thus discourage judgment and discretion? Slavish compliance is required when controls are designed and enforced without rationality, without need, and without consideration for the sensitivities of the people affected by them. Then they become more honored in the breach than in the observance. Covert and overt resistance can follow. In fact, in some organizational settings, overcontrol often results in petty acts of fraud and thievery (e.g., lying on expense accounts and fudging performance data) as methods of rebellion.

How can one overcome resistance to or negative reactions to controls?

1. Make sure that goals, objectives, and control standards are realistic, not impossible or improbable to achieve. Standards, goals, and objectives should be challenging but attainable with ordinary, not extraordinary, effort.

2. Involve in the control-setting process the employees who will be bound by the standards.

3. Install controls only where they are necessary for the practice of prudent management, and evaluate their continued need and enhancement periodically. The real enemies to good and effective controls are undercontrol and overcontrol.

4. Tight controls are fine as long as their administration and monitoring are placed as far down in the organization as possible. (Otherwise, the brass gets too bogged down in detail-and-control trivia, and lower-level managers become more and more like police officers.)

5. Give output controls a slight edge over behavior controls as methodologies (i.e., monitor the quantity and quality of output against the present standard). Behavior controls (i.e., personal observations) are best used when performance requirements are clear and generally known; here, surveillance is perceived as less obtrusive. In fact, if coupled with positive reinforcements, such surveillance can promote efficiency and motivation. So both output and behavior controls play important roles in achieving organizational objectives.

6. New and better controls do not of themselves solve problems. But together with enlightened management, good administration, and intelligent interpretation, controls lead to efficient and effective operations.

7. Controls can be of two types: before the fact and after the fact. Before-the-fact controls are intended to prevent problems from occurring. They pinpoint violations of established policies and procedures and spot

errors in input accuracy and validity. After-the-fact controls are intended to detect problems that may quickly grow out of control and require immediate remedies.

8. Finally, rules are complied with when they are fair, rational, and needed for orderly procedure.

REFERENCES

1. *SEC vs. AM International, Inc.*, Civil action No. 83-1256, D.D.C. (May 2, 1983) Litigation Release No. 9980, February 27, 1984.

4

FRAUD AUDITING IN A COMPUTER ENVIRONMENT

A computer-related crime in very broad terms means a crime in which a computer is used as a means or instrument to commit or abet a crime, or a crime in which a computer itself is the victim. The usual crimes committed by computer include embezzlement, theft of property and proprietary information, fraud, forgery, and counterfeiting. Crimes committed against computers include sabotage, vandalism, and electronic wiretapping, that is, gaining illegal access by impersonating an authorized user, or exceeding one's own authority.

Computer-related crime can be looked at as a phenomenon brought about by advances in information-processing technologies. In that sense it is a technological phenomenon. Before we had computers, we had no computer crime. But before we had computers we did have crime—both the white-and blue-collar varieties. We also had crimes of violence (crimes against people) and crimes against property. The computer did not usher in a new wave of crime. It merely changed the form of older crimes. Embezzlers can now steal by making electronic entries in books of account rather than pen and ink or electro-mechanical entries.

Computer-related crime today is an occupational crime; that is, it is committed mainly by people with the requisite skills, knowledge, and access. Access can be gained more easily by organizational insiders (employees) than by outsiders (intruders, hackers). Therefore insiders represent a greater potential computer crime threat than do outsiders, irrespective of the opinions of mass media commentators, who often suggest the opposite.

One might therefore conclude that computer-related crime is a phenomenon that involves knowledgeable people with questionable dispositions. But that also is too simple to be true. The idea that criminals are born crime prone has not won much favor from behavioral scientists. They suggest that cultural and environmental conditioning are more significant factors in understanding crime.

We shall therefore look at the phenomenon of computer-related crime from a number of perspectives:

1. The individual criminal, and his or her motivations
2. The external environmental factors that exacerbate motivations to commit computer crime
3. The internal organizational cultures that minimize or maximize the probability of such crimes

4.1 THE HISTORY AND EVOLUTION OF COMPUTER-RELATED CRIMES

Electronic computers were first introduced for commercial use in the United States in the mid-1950s. Before that time the few computers that existed were used for governmental purposes (i.e., for the tabulation of the national census, for military applications, and for scientific research). It is evident, therefore, that we had no computer-related crimes before we had computers. So the history of the computer crime begins in the mid-1950s.

Until 1958 no systematic tracking or tabulation of computer-related crime existed. In 1958 Stanford Research International (SRI) began tracking publicly reported incidents of computer abuse, some of which were criminal and others that involved the breach of civil laws such as the copyright and patent acts. SRI grouped these incidents into four categories:

1. Vandalism (against computers)
2. Information or property theft
3. Financial fraud or theft
4. Unauthorized use or sale of (computer) services

The first year in which 10 or more of the above incident types were reported was 1968. There were a total of 13 incidents that year. Reported incidents thereafter were as follows:

Year	Total Incidents
1969	20
1970	38
1971	59
1972	72
1973	76
1974	74
1975	81
1976	57
1977	85
1978	31

Stanford Research discontinued tabulating such abuses after 1978 for several reasons. First the publicly reported incidents bore no relationship to all incidents. Many, perhaps most, incidents of computer abuse were not publicly reported. So tabulating reported incidents by year could create the impression that computer abuse was growing or declining when in fact the reported incidents might not be fairly representative of all actual incidents of abuse. Also, with more and more computers being used, one could expect an increase in the number of incidents of abuse. Second, tabulating reported incidents of abuse would shed no light on the phenomenon itself or its causative factors. So SRI elected to look at each case individually for whatever insights it could glean on causations and other variables, such as the mental dispositions of the computer abusers and the employment conditions that made abuse more likely—demographic characteristics of abusers.

Now a word on what we do know about computer-related fraud versus what the mass public has assumed to be true. The current computer-crime phenomenon is not significantly different from what businesses experienced 30 years ago. There is no conclusive evidence that the current rate of insider computer-related business crimes, such as employee theft, fraud, and embezzlement, is greater than it was in the past. But computing systems are more vulnerable to outsider attack by way of electronic eavesdropping and other illegal-access methods.

We can therefore sum up our theory of computer-related crime in a concept we call MOMM, an acronymn for motivations, opportunities, means, and methods.

Motivations (Who and Why)
   Economic
   Ideological
   Egocentric
   Psychotic
Opportunities (What, When and Where)
   Inadequate Systems Controls
      Accounting Controls
      Access Controls
   Inadequacies in Management Controls
      Reward System
      Ethical Climate
      Climate for Trust
Means (How)
   Compromising Controls
   Compromising Personnel
   Compromising Technology
Methods (How much, How often)
   Input Scams
   Throughput Scams
   Output Scams

We can then depict computer-related theft as an iterative process. (Exhibit 4.1).

The personal motives that can lead to the commission of a computer crime are:

1. Economic
2. Egocentric
3. Ideological
4. Psychotic

✶   Economic motives would indicate the perpetrator has as a main purpose a need or desire to secure a financial gain from his crime— money or things that can be disposed of for money.

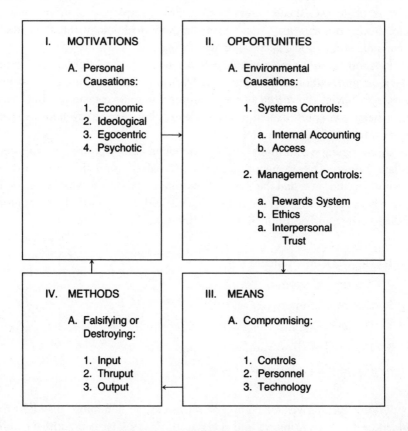

EXHIBIT 4.1. The Computer Theft Iteration

Egocentric motives mean a need or desire to show off the perpetrator's talent in committing what the general public tends to see as a complex crime. Stealing money may be included in the criminal act but it is not the primary purpose of the act. The stolen funds are a secondary consideration—the more the better, but only to demonstrate the prowess of the perpetrator. Youthful hackers usually fall into this category. Their intentions are not generally to steal money but to elicit information so they can demonstrate how bright they are.

Ideological motives are demonstrated when the perpetrator feels impelled to seek revenge against someone or something he believes is oppressing or exploiting him. Terrorist bombings of computer centers exemplify that mindset. Sabotage against computers by disgruntled employees is another example. Such criminals may think that computer technology threatens their economic and political survival or well-being.

Psychotic motives include a distorted sense of reality, delusions of grandeur, or persecution and exaggerated fears of computers, to a point where bizarre behavior is directed against computers to relieve anxieties. But there have been few reported incidents of computer abuse where psychotic motives were attributed to perpetrators.

Environmental conditions that have provided motive power for computer-related crime and abuse include both the internal environment of the firm that operates a computer and the external environment (i.e., the world or marketplace in general). Internal influences that can add to the motive for computer-related crime and abuse include such things as:

1. The work environment
2. The reward system
3. The level of interpersonal trust
4. The level of ethics
5. The level of stress (pressure for performance)
6. The level of internal controls

Externally, motives for computer-related crime and abuse may be provided by the current mores and social values of society, competitive conditions in the industry, and economic conditions in the country or the world.

Computer-related crimes can be grouped into three categories that parallel the three stages of data processing: input tampering, throughput tampering, and output tampering. (We owe this classification to Robert Jacobson, a well-known computer security consultant in New York City.) Input crimes involve the entry of false or fraudulent data into a computer (i.e., data that have been altered, forged, or counterfeited—raised, lowered, destroyed, intentionally omitted, or fabricated). Input scams are probably the most common computer-related crimes and yet perhaps the easiest kind to prevent with effective supervision and controls (such as separation of duties and proper audit trails).

Throughput crimes require a knowledge of programming. Such colorful expressions as salami slicing, trojan horses, trap doors, time bombs, and logic bombs have been used to describe these computer abuses. The publicly reported cases of such abuses are far fewer than the input crimes mentioned earlier. If it is true that computer crimes, like most white-collar crimes, are economically motivated, then it would seem reasonable to assume the incident rate of throughput scams will be lower than input scams and output scams, because the chief culprits of these latter two types of computer crimes are data entry clerks and computer operators who earn considerably less than programmers and analysts.

Output crimes, such as theft of computer-generated reports and information files (customer mailing lists, R & D results, long-range plans, employee lists, secret formulas, etc.) seem to be increasing in this era of intense competition, particularly among high technology manufacturers.

Among the publicly reported cases of computer crime, most have been of the input and output type and have involved lower-level data processing clerks—entry clerks and computer operators. However, because throughput crimes are more difficult to detect, we cannot say that their number is exceeded by the other two types. We simply do not know. Furthermore, throughput crimes may not be reported for other reasons as well; proving them is quite complex, and admitting that they even occurred is an embarrassment to top management.

4.2 THE MOST COMMON COMPUTER-RELATED CRIMES

Whereas computer hacking (electronic break-ins of mainframe computers by pranksters) has received most of the recent media attention, the most prevalent computer crime has been the fraudulent disbursement of funds that is generally preceded by the submission of a spurious claim in the following forms:

1. False vendor, supplier, or contractor invoice
2. False governmental benefit claim
3. False fringe benefit claim
4. False refund or credit claim
5. False payroll claim
6. False expense claim

Fraudulent disbursement of funds usually requires a data entry clerk in accounts payable, payroll, or the benefits sections, either acting alone or in collusion with an insider or outsider (depending on how tight the internal controls are). From an accountant's perspective, the claim is a false debit to an expense, so that a corresponding credit can be posted to the cash account for the issuance of a check. Auditors assert such disbursement frauds represent more than half of all frauds by lower-level employees.

At higher levels of management, the typical fraud involves the overstatement of profits by the fabrication of such data as sales, which are increased arbitrarily or by artifice (sales booked before the sales transaction is completed), and the understatement of expenses, which are arbitrarily reduced or disguised as deferrals to the next accounting period. There are numerous variations on these two main themes—overstatement of sales and understatement of expenses. One of the more common ploys to overstate profits is to arbitrarily increase the ending inventory of manufactured goods or merchandise held for sale. That ploy results in understating the cost of goods sold and thereby increases the net profit.

The incentive to overstate profits is often brought about by the executive compensation system. If bonus awards depend on profits, executives have an economic incentive to fudge the numbers. They may also be tempted to do so if they own a great deal of company stock whose value depends on investor perceptions of profitability. If profits are down, investors are not happy and may rush to sell, thus causing a lowering of the stock's price and depressing the value of the executive's own stock.

Manipulations of the above type often require the joining of both line executives and personnel in accounting and data processing capacities. We saw such an example in the Equity Funding case, and we have seen many others since that time. Such conspiracies are becoming a recurring theme in business. The pressure on executives for high performance grows with each passing year. We are therefore likely to see more of such frauds in the future.

4.3 THE NATURE OF COMPUTER-RELATED CRIME

Crimes like embezzlement and employee thefts of funds were not unheard of before computers came into being. Accountants attempted to discourage such crimes by requiring that a separation of duties exist between persons who handled cash or other assets and those who made entries in the books of account. Accessibility to assets and accountability for the recording of transactions concerning such assets were thereby divided, on the theory that requiring two persons to conspire to commit a theft of assets would reduce the probability of such a theft.

An added control measure instituted by accountants was called the paper trail or audit trail. In essence that control measure required that all business transactions be entered into journals and be supported by paper documents (i.e., vendor invoices, purchase orders, receiving reports, canceled checks, disbursement vouchers, sales receipts, or customer invoices) before disbursement could be made.

But despite these control measures, employee thefts, frauds, and embezzlements were still possible. Accounting systems were not designed to be foolproof or fraud proof. A determined defrauder could still find ways to circumvent or override controls even in the manual era of accounting. Computers have not changed that human disposition. Fraud, thefts, and embezzlements are still possible in the computer era.

4.4 COMPUTER CRIME: A SELECTED CASE AWARENESS FOR THE FRAUD AUDITOR

Coauthor Bologna's organization, Computer Protection Systems, Inc., has for the past several years published a monthly newsletter called the "Computer Security Digest." That newsletter provides the selected information on computer crime that follows.[1]

Issue Date	Computer Crime Victim
June 1982	University of Maryland

Details: A computer operator at the University of Maryland hospital was charged with embezzling $40,000 by submitting false invoices. . . [that] were processed through the hospital's computer. The same hospital's former assistant D/P [data processing] manager accepted a $41,000 bribe from a D/P consultant and conspired with another D/P consultant to steal $126,000 from the hospital by submitting false invoices for software devices. Both the operator and the assistant D/P manager had previous convictions for D/P-related crime! The hospital did not, as a matter of course, conduct background investigations on D/P employment applicants.

Issue Date	Computer Crime Victim
June 1982	Magnetic Peripherals

Details: A subsidiary of Control Data Corp. was another victim of computer crime. An accounts payable terminal operator at Magnetic Peripherals and her boyfriend conspired to defraud the company by fabricating invoices from a fictitious vendor. Five checks totaling $155,000 were then issued to the vendor, after which the terminal operator and her boyfriend left for a sunnier climate. The operator turned herself in a year later and disclosed the fraud to police because her boyfriend tried to effectuate a reconciliation with his estranged wife.

Issue Date	Computer Crime Victim
September 1982	Bank of New England

Details: A Boston federal grand jury indicted a former supervisor in the Bank of New England's proof-and-control department for embezzling $30,000. The bank provided custodial and record-keeping services for a number of investment companies, over which the accused had some responsibility. The indictment charged that he substituted his own name or account number for those of the actual buyers of shares in the funds. He then used the computerized record-keeping and correction system to conceal the imbalances and avoid detection. [This is another illustration of an "input" scam, (i.e., altering or fabricating computer input or deceiving the computer.)] One possible defense against bank employee scams of this type might be to keep employee accounts (loans and deposits) segregated from customer accounts. Any intergroup transfer (customer to employee or vice versa) could then be flagged for audit or exception-reporting purposes.

Issue	Computer Crime Victim
October 1982	Texaco

Details: A former EDP employee of Texaco, Inc., and his wife were indicted for stealing $18,000 from the company in an accounts payable-type fraud. The employee instructed Texaco's computer to pay his wife rent for land she allegedly leased to Texaco by assigning her an alphanumeric code as a lessor and then ordering that payments be made. (The lesson here is simple: *never* let a data entry clerk in accounts payable, who processes payment claims, also have access to the approved vendor master file for additions or deletions. Doing otherwise violates the separation-of-duties principle of internal controls.)

Issue	Computer Crime Victim
January 1983	Bank of America and Merrill Lynch

Details: Bank of America and Merrill Lynch were the joint victims of a computer fraud engineered by insiders at both firms which involved the unauthorized reprogramming of the Bank of America computer in a scheme to defraud it and Merrill Lynch of $200,000. A computer operator for the Bank of America was arrested as a co-conspirator with a Merrill Lynch insider. The scheme involved the Bank of America computer operator gaining access to a terminal and inflating the balances of three accounts held by a Merrill Lynch customer, a co-conspirator. The Merrill Lynch insider then modified records at that firm to show that funds in the customer's account were disburseable [sic] (though based on bogus checks issued on the Bank of America inflated accounts). The scheme did not accomplish its desired results because the Bank of America's programming controls were tight enough to identify both the terminal and operator making programming checks. Only $17,000 was stolen before the plot was discovered.

Issue Date	Computer Crime Violation
April 1983	Slavenburg Bank

Details: Slavenburg Bank, Rotterdam, Netherlands. Rob Vander Heul, 33, head of the foreign transfer department and his assistant, T. Aard, were arrested on suspicion of forgery and embezzlement for a scheme that involved the taking of at least $65 million over a two-year period. Police believe the money was embezzled by breaking the bank's computer code allowing funds to be funneled into outside accounts. The alleged fraud was discovered through audit. The bank's management is also under investigation for tax evasion.

Issue Date	Computer Crime Victim
June 1983	Washington State

Details: A Washington programmer/analyst whose job was to develop safeguards to prevent vocational counselors and data entry operators from gaining unauthorized access to the state's system pleaded guilty to stealing almost $17,000. Most of the money was used to buy drinks at a local bar. A small amount of the money was given to friends who needed financial assistance. The money was stolen from a fund that was designed to train the handicapped for new careers. Other interesting case points: (1) the program which was used to steal the money was also apparently designed to erase automatically all evidence of his illegal transactions from the system's files; and (2) the discovery of the crime occurred by accident when an accountant noticed that an address on a "remittance advice" was identical to the programmer's home address.

Issue Date	Computer Crime Victim
June 1983	Connecticut General Insurance

Details: A benefit analyst with Connecticut General Insurance used her remote terminal in a Dade County, Florida, field claims office to defraud the company of $206,000 between April 1981 and January 1983. Case highlights: (1) she used her position of trust and knowledge of the claims system to execute the fraud; and (2) she used false names to submit fictitious claims but used the addresses of herself, her father, and her boyfriend. The repetition of the same claimant addresses eventually tipped off the insurance company's security department.

Issue Date	Computer Crime Victim
July 1983	Eastern Michigan University

Details: On December 19, 1982, Eastern Michigan University's computer system was accessed by one or more people who damaged nearly 43,000 student records stored on the system. Many student's first names were changed to "Susan." Student telephone numbers were replaced with the phone number of the university's president, grade point averages were modified, and some academic files were deleted completely. The university's outside auditors, Arthur Young and Co., reported that the computer's security system was penetrated either by someone who had extensive knowledge of the system or by misuse of the password used by the admissions office.

Issue Date	Computer Crime Victim
July 1983	Michigan Department of Social Services

Details: A former Michigan Department of Social Services computer operator was charged with programming a computer to send more than $10,000 in welfare checks and food stamps to her family, a friend, and herself. They were charged with welfare fraud, computer fraud, forgery, and related violations.

Issue Date	Computer Crime Victim
July 1983	Southeastern Michigan Transportation Authority

Details: A 31-year old Detroit bus scheduler was acquitted of criminal charges involving extortion and violation of Michigan's 1980 computer-crime law. The scheduler who developed seven report generation programs for the Southeastern Michigan Transportation Authority (SEMTA) attempted to collect $19,500 in payment for the programs after he was fired. The programs were developed with built-in security access blocks which made accessing the source code difficult. The scheduler was said to have demanded the $19,500 before he would turn over the access codes needed to alter the source code. The programs were developed over a two-year period in his free time. The scheduler's attorney contended that the programs saved approximately $150,000 over the past two years.

Issue Date	Computer Crime Victim
August 1983	Northampton County, Pennsylvania

Details: A computer operator employed by the Northampton County, Pennsylvania, Domestic Relations Department was charged with embezzling $84,000. The operator claimed she used the funds to pay for illegal drugs for her boyfriend. She had access to both cash and accounting records and used a "cash lapping" technique to withdraw funds. When apprehended she demonstrated the technique to her superiors to avoid its occurrence in the future. (Another classic case of not maintaining a separation of duties. Letting the same employee handle both money and the journal entry for recording the receipt of the money is a real no-no. It isn't lax control. It's *no* control.)

Issue	Computer Crime Victim
August 1983	Collins Food International Inc.

Details: Criminal charges were filed against Dennis Williams, 30, and Michael Lampert, 22, former employees of Collins Foods International, Inc. The two allegedly programmed "logic bombs" that would erase inventory and payroll information processed by the company for 400 Kentucky Fried Chicken franchises and Sizzler Family Steak Houses. The programmed commands, one of which was set to activate on June 7, would have also shut down the computer system and erased all traces of the destructive commands. The motive is still unknown.

Issue	Computer Crime Victim
January 1984	National Bio-Analytical Clinical Labs

Details: A computer programmer for National Bio-Analytical Clinical Laboratories, Farmington Hills, Michigan (now out of business), was found guilty of 46 counts of mail fraud. In 1981 he had submitted $171,000 in fraudulent claims to Blue Cross and Blue Shield of Michigan.

Issue	Computer Crime Victim
January 1984	Aetna Life and Casualty Company

Details: A former Aetna Life (Toledo, Ohio) customer relations representative was sentenced to a six-month prison term for using a computer to issue more than $8,000 in fraudulent dental insurance benefit checks. The checks were issued to her relatives, who were also charged. The criminal charge used to prosecute the case was mail fraud. (This is another case of input manipulation.) *Note*: After the fraud was discovered, she perpetrated a similar scheme at her next employment.

Issue	Computer Crime Victim
January 1984	California Welfare Department

Details: Although the exact amount of loss sustained by the Alameda County, California, Welfare Department is unknown, it is quite evident that over $300,000 has been lost due to fraud committed by a supervisor and clerk. Again this is a case of an input falsification fraud. A welfare department compliance unit supervisor and one of her clerks falsified dozens of welfare claims over a period of a year and collected unauthorized payments for the claims. The two were caught when one of the welfare department's data entry clerks discovered incomplete information on an input document authorizing a claim payment. The clerk then checked with the eligibility worker whose name had been forged on the document. When the eligibility worker denied authorizing the claim or signing the document, an investigation was launched.

Issue	Computer Crime Victim
February 1984	Japanese Bank Case

Details: Embezzlement, in Japan: A 32-year old bank clerk, at her lover's request, opened a number of savings accounts under assumed names in some of the bank's branch offices. She accumulated over $500,000 by channeling funds into the accounts by entering "receipt money" transactions into the bank's computer system. Six months after she withdrew the money, international investigators arrested her in the Philippines.

Issue	Computer Crime Victim
February 1984	Australia Betting Agency Case

Details: A *Computerworld* article reports that an operator at a state-run horse betting agency changed the time clock in the computer system by three minutes. After a race was run, the operator would quickly telephone his girlfriend, an input clerk, and give her the winning horses and the amounts to bet. Loss: unknown. Detected: when his girlfriend got angry because he left her for another woman.

Issue	Computer Crime Victim
February 1984	West Germany Payroll Case

Details: Embezzlement, in West Germany: A programmer used a payroll scam to embezzle $75,000 from his employer. He developed a payroll program that would change the payroll transactions so that they would never appear on any master list or his wage slips. Detected: by chance.

Issue	Computer Crime Victim
May 1984	New York City Law Firm Case

Details: Two employees of the New York City law firm of Skadden, Arps, Slate, Meagher, & Flom and an unemployed broker were charged with conspiracy to illegally trade in securities by the U.S. Securities and Exchange Commission. The law firm's employees, a proofreader and a word processor operator, apparently deciphered the meaning of internal office codes contained on the firm's word processing system and gained access to information on tender offers and corporate acquisition plans. The information was passed on to others including an unemployed broker in exchange for a share of the profits gained. One of the illegal insider trading schemes netted $60,000 to the conspirators.

Issue	Computer Crime Victim
February 1985	Texas Programmer Case

Details: A 24-year old self-employed programmer was charged with the theft of $100,000 in what Harris County (Houston) authorities said was a high-tech fraud involving the illegal access of the Greater Houston Credit Bureau's computerized records. Case highlights: The culprit allegedly accessed the credit history of 38 affluent local residents. He then used their names and credit information to acquire 76 Mastercard and Visa cards from the First City Bank in Dallas. These cards were then used to issue himself $100,000 from a number of Automatic Teller Machines.

Issue	Computer Crime Victim
December 1985	San Diego Hackers

Details: FBI agents seized 25 microcomputer systems from San Diego area teens who allegedly accessed Interactive Data Corporation's computer. Interactive Data, a subsidiary of Chase Manhattan Corp., maintains Chase's financial records and is located in Waltham, Massachusetts. Case highlights: Those involved in the unauthorized access were 23 teenagers, ages 13 to 17. Apparently no money was taken or transferred from accounts. The youths changed a number of passwords that prevented authorized access to accounts. One fictitious account was created. Files were destroyed or modified. The hackers threatened to destroy records unless they were given free access to the system. The investigation began when Interactive Data found that several unsuccessful attempts were made to enter Chase's records via a toll-free number used by qualified system users. The unauthorized phone calls to the computer were traced by the FBI.

Issue	Computer Crime Victim
March 1986	Washington State Hacker

Details: A Kirkland, Washington 18-year-old admitted accessing the computers of four Seattle-area companies, including Microsoft Corp. Case highlights:

The hacker apparently could issue payroll checks at one company and could establish new accounts and passwords locking out system operators at several others. Files were copied. Police seized several computers and more than 300 diskettes from the hacker's home. Also confiscated were a list of credit card numbers with owner's card numbers, names, and expiration dates; printouts of information from Microsoft; directions and access codes to dial up the credit report agency. The hacker admitted checking some 50,000 telephone numbers for modem tones.

4.5 THE VALUE OF STORED DATA

With the advent of the computers a new form of asset has been created: the data held in the computer. The data may eventually cause money to change hands as in EFT systems. Although the data is not a negotiable instrument (as is a bank check), it nonetheless has a value attached to it. Further examples of these assets are bank-to-bank transfers, accounts receivable balances, inventory levels, funds-and-deposit balances, fixed assets listings, and accounts payable balances. Other more intangible assets include valued or confidential programs, scientific data files, programs sold commercially by a company for a profit, confidential financial information, computer time, and so on.

4.6 COMPUTER COMMUNICATIONS

Computer communications may be defined here as the ability to transfer messages between independent hardware devices. In order to communicate, the computer devices must, of course, be connected in some way. A network refers to the computer, the terminals, and any other peripheral devices that are interconnected.

The idea of connecting computers is not new. It has been possible for a number of years to sit down at terminals that are in the same building as the mainframe computer to which the terminals are linked, or at remote terminals hundreds of miles from the mainframe computer, and send data back and forth between the terminals and the mainframe. Most computers of any size have one or more terminals attached to them (sometimes hundreds) and are part of a network. Terminals can communicate with the central or host computer via either telephone lines or dedicated data telecommunication lines.

The terminal may function simply as an input/output device enabling its user to run programs on the central computer. A terminal that cannot do any processing itself is called a *dumb* terminal. *Intelligent* or *smart* terminals, on the other hand, can process data downloaded from the central computer because they have their own software.

Terminals can communicate not only with the organization's own large computers but with external computers—computers owned by service bureaus or computers containing data bases that the public can access for a fee, such as Info Globe or Compu-Service. Besides bibliographic information, public data bases offer a wide variety of services to users, such as financial, stock market, and other statistical information; travel information, and access to electronic bulletin boards.

The network scene has become more complicated in recent years with the arrival of microcomputers in the workplace. Although most of the microcomputers now in use are "standalones" (i.e., they function completely independently), microcomputer users sooner or later are likely to communicate with each other and with the organization's central computer to share information and programs. The need to communicate has spurred the development of local area networks (LANs).

A LAN is a data communications system that links one or more independent services (microcomputers, printers, hard disks) and enables them to communicate. The LAN transmits data over short distances and is usually confined to a small area such as a department (one floor), a single building, or a warehouse. Cabling is used to link the equipment together.

Microcomputers may be linked to other microcomputers in a LAN, or they may be linked to the central computer via a wide-area network, or both. They can then function as independent workstations, or they can operate in conjunction with the other hardware devices that are on the LAN, or they can function as terminals to the central computer.

4.7 CHARACTERISTICS OF THE COMPUTER ENVIRONMENT

Although computerized accounting systems are a natural progression from manual accounting systems, they do have special characteristics that make them more susceptible to criminal activity or abuse. In order to understand the potential impact and extent of computer-related crime, it is necessary to understand these characteristics.

4.7.1 Data Is Concentrated in One Place

Computer systems collect and combine data, usually from all departments within an organization. This information is processed and centrally stored. This centralization means that the data is in one location and therefore all data in that location is vulnerable to abuse. By simply obtaining the appropriate password, a person could access any or all of a company's financial or other records.

4.7.2 The Medium of Storage Is Vulnerable

Assets are widely recorded in magnetic form. This medium of storage is volatile and easily abused. The stored information is vulnerable.

4.7.3 The Audit Trail May Be Obscure

The sheer volume of transactions, together with the on-line access and networks available on many systems, may result in confused or incomplete audit trails.

4.7.4 Visible Records May Be Nonexistent

Permanent records are often stored in machine-readable form. Any abuse of these records, whether data or actual programs, is therefore less likely to be detected by nonspecialists. In addition, a theft or other form of abuse may remain undetected for a long time, allowing the perpetrator to cover his tracks or disappear.

4.7.5 Programs and Data Can Be Altered Without Leaving a Trace of the Alteration

Manual records may reveal tampering or alterations, whereas computer records stored on a magnetic medium may be altered by writing over a record obliterating the previous record without leaving any trail as to the source of the change.

4.7.6 Tampering Can Be Carried Out Almost Instantly

Computers cannot discriminate between legitimate and illegitimate users once any security system in place has been breached. The computer will change data instantly when commanded to do so. Its speed means that a computer criminal is at risk only briefly while actually committing the crime and is much less likely to be caught in the act.

4.7.7 Networks Increase the Risks

As mentioned earlier, networks increase the vulnerability of computer systems. Information can be stolen by copying it through a workstation or by tapping into transmission cables. Unauthorized entry can be gained through public telephone lines. Information may be downloaded from a highly secure central computer to a microcomputer whose operator then leaves the floppy disk containing the information unattended on a desktop. The more terminals there are, the more opportunities there are to gain unauthorized access to the central computer.

4.7.8 Computer Systems Are Not Widely Understood

Computer systems are in some ways becoming more and more complex as technology advances. It requires considerable expertise to understand what is happening in a computer environment, especially with regard to computer programs. Thus abuses are not as likely to be detected as other types of crimes.

4.7.9 Security Features Are Not Always Built in

Much of the hardware and many of the operating systems in use today were designed without much thought being given to the prevention of computer abuse or crime.

4.7.10 Internal Control Features May Be Inadequate

Many computer analysts and programmers are not knowledgeable about accounting controls or the general principles of internal control. As a result, some systems are designed without adequate controls in the first place. In addition, many programs that have been operating for a long time have undergone extensive changes. The changes may be poorly documented and the "patched" programs little understood. Anyone with sufficient knowledge of programming could conceivably manipulate or change the programs to his or her benefit without a change being discovered.

4.7.11 Trusted Personnel May Circumvent Controls

Programmers and data entry clerks are in a position to manipulate records by the very nature of their jobs. A high degree of trust has to be reposed in them, and a corresponding degree of risk exists for the organization.

Technicial personnel may be able to get around built-in controls, or they may deliberately exploit a flaw discovered in the course of their work. Disgruntled employees, or employees who enjoy seeing the computer "tripped up," may also abuse computer systems. Finally, managers may override normal controls built into the system.

4.8 COMPUTER SYSTEM THREATS

There are three main categories of threats to computer systems:

1. Theft, including theft of assets, data and programs
2. Manipulation, including the additions or deletions of information contained in data files or programs
3. Theft of computer time

Some examples of fraudulent activities that may be employed are:

1. Adding, deleting, or changing input data, or entering fraudulent data
2. Misposting or partially posting transactions
3. Producing counterfeit output, or suppressing, destroying, or stealing output
4. Tampering with programs (e.g., to take money from many accounts in small amounts)
5. Altering or deleting master files, or holding them for ransom
6. Overriding internal controls to gain access to confidential information
7. Exploiting intersystem deficiencies
8. Committing sabotage
9. Stealing computer time
10. Conducting electronic surveillance of data as it is transmitted
11. Browsing or insider hacking (i.e., probing into the data base)

Besides these and other threats, computerized accounting systems are vulnerable to all the dangers inherent in any accounting system whether computerized or manual.

REFERENCES

1. Jack Bologna, Computer Security Digest, 1982–1984 issues.

PART TWO

AN AWARENESS OF FORENSIC AND INVESTIGATIVE ACCOUNTING

5

WHAT IS FORENSIC AND INVESTIGATIVE ACCOUNTING?

Although a relatively new discipline to the accounting profession, the role of a forensic expert from other professions has been in place for some time. The Webster's Dictionary defines the word *forensic* as "belonging to, used in, or suitable to courts of judicature or to public discussions and debate" and the term *forensic medicine* as "a science that deals with the relation and application of medical facts to legal problems." Accordingly the term *forensic* is applicable to the accounting profession as a discipline that deals with the relation and application of financial facts to legal problems. Quite often at the mention of the word *forensic* the listener draws a criminal reference, however, this is attributable to the tendency of the press to report criminal cases more than civil matters. Consistent with the above definition, forensic accounting evidence is oriented to a court of law whether that court is criminal or civil. Furthermore, with the orientation to the court of law, a standard is immediately established as to the quality of the work the forensic accountant must attain as his or her findings are subject to public scrutiny should the matter at issue go to trial. For the accounting and most other professions, the possibility of public scrutiny makes the forensic application unique.

The involvement of the forensic accountant is almost always on a reactive basis, which distinguishes the forensic accountant from the fraud auditor, who more usually tends to be involved on an active basis with the aspects of prevention and detection in a corporate or regulatory environment. The forensic accountant is trained to react to complaints arising in criminal matters; statements of claim arising in civil litigation; rumors and inquiries arising in corporate investigations. At all times the investigative findings of the forensic accountant will have an impact on an individual and/or a company in terms of either freedom or financial award/loss.

The forensic accountant draws on various resources to obtain all relevant financial evidence and to interpret and present this evidence in a manner that will assist both parties. Ideally, forensic accounting should allow two parties to more quickly and efficiently resolve the complaint, statement of claim, rumor, inquiry or at least reduce the financial element as an area of ongoing debate.

5.1 WHO NEEDS FORENSIC ACCOUNTING?

The increased business complexities in a litigious environment has enhanced the need for this discipline. It is possible to summarize the range of application into the following general areas:

1. Corporate Investigations. Companies react to concerns that arise through a number of sources that might suggest possible wrongdoing within and without the corporate environment. From the anonymous phone call/ letter to disgruntled employees and third parties these problems must be addressed in a timely and effective manner in order to permit the company to continue to pursue its objectives. More specifically, the forensic accountant would provide assistance in addressing such allegations ranging from kickbacks and wrongful dismissals to internal situations involving allegations of management/employee wrongdoing. At times the involvement of a forensic accountant can be advantageous in meeting with those persons affected by the allegations, rumors, or inquiries as they may view the accountant as an independent and objective party, and be more willing to engage in discussion.

2. Litigation Support. Litigation support includes assistance to counsel in the investigation and assessment of the integrity and quantum of issues relating to such areas as loss of profits, construction claims, product liability, shareholder disputes, and breach of contract.

3. Criminal Matters. White-collar crime has consistently involved accountants and auditors in attempting to sort out, assess, and report on financial transactions related to allegations against individuals and companies in a

variety of situations, such as arson, shams, fraud, kickbacks, and stock market manipulations. In criminal matters there is an increased importance in the role of the accountant/auditor as an expert witness in presenting his or her findings in court.

4. Insurance Claims. Both the preparation and assessment of insurance claims on behalf of the insured and insurers may require the assistance of a forensic accountant to assess both the integrity and quantum of a claim. The more significant areas relate to the calculation of loss arising from business interruption, fidelity bond, and personal injury matters. Whereas certain of these cases require financial projections, many have a need for historical analysis upon which the future projections can be based.

5. Government. The forensic accountant can assist governments with regulatory compliance by ensuring that the appropriate legislation is being followed by companies subject to same. Grants and subsidy investigations and public inquiries form a part of this government assistance.

In generalizing the type of situation that creates a need for the forensic accountant, it might be suggested that the forensic accountant is required when there is a potential perceived or real financial loss or risk of loss. It is the responsibility of the forensic accountant to, in effect, be a problem solver.

5.2 WHAT SHOULD A FORENSIC ACCOUNTANT BE ABLE TO DO?

The knowledge of one's accounting profession is a given. It is the expertise unique to a forensic accountant that must be acquired over time, through practical experience and training, which enables the forensic accountant to be of assistance in addressing the areas noted earlier. The forensic accountant will have an understanding of the court system and an awareness of various legal terminology and documents and the rules of evidence. He or she will also understand the various concepts that come into play, be it the determination of a pattern of conduct in a fraudulent situation or the determination of future loss of profits arising out of a personal injury situation. Familiarity with the intricacies of policy agreements in the insurance industry, to various types of governmental legislation, all become part of the knowledge base of the forensic accountant. In addition to this academic approach is the experience gained through actual cases where one brings judgment to bear on issues and decisions. In essence forensic skills are summarized as follows:

1. **Identification of Financial Issues.** When the forensic accountant is presented with a situation generated by a complaint, allegation, rumor, inquiry or statement of claim it is important that the forensic accountant clearly identify the financial issues significant to the matter in a timely fashion. This decision is based on experience and knowledge. Any recommendations resulting from this decision must reflect common sense and business reality. For example, if documents are needed from a foreign jurisdiction, whereas it may be the most obvious recommendation to obtain these records, it is usually not the most practical. Other alternatives must be considered.

2. **Knowledge of Investigative Techniques.** When the issues have been identified it is imperative that further information and documentation be acquired in order to obtain further evidence that would assist one to either support or refute the allegation or claim. Not only is it a question of knowing where the relevant financial documentation exists, but also the intricacies of generally accepted accounting principles, financial statement disclosure, systems of internal control, and an awareness of the human element within the operation of a company.

3. **Knowledge of Evidence.** The forensic accountant must understand what constitutes evidence, the meaning of "best" and "primary" evidence, and the form that various accounting summaries can take to consolidate the financial evidence in a way acceptable to the courts.

4. **Interpretation of Financial Information.** It is unusual for a transaction or a series of events to have only one interpretation. The forensic accountant must be extremely conscious of a natural bias that can exist in the interpretation process. It is important that transactions are viewed from all aspects to ensure that the ultimate interpretation of the available information fits with common sense and the test of business reality. A proper interpretation of information can only be assured when one has looked behind and beyond the transaction in question without any scope limitations.

5. **Presentation of Findings.** The forensic accountant must have the ability to clearly communicate the findings resulting from the investigation in an understandable fashion to the layperson. The presentation can be oral or written and can include the appropriate demonstrative aids. The role of the

forensic accountant in the witness box is the final test of his or her findings in a public forum.

5.2.1 Investigative Concerns

Investigative concerns exist and must be addressed by the forensic accountant at the appropriate time during the course of his or her investigation. For example, in dealing with criminal matters the primary concern is to develop evidence around motive, opportunity, and benefit. Of equal concern is that the benefit of doubt is given to the other side to ensure that proper interpretations are given to the transactions. Other concerns such as the question of method of operation and the issue of economic risk must also be addressed.

Similarly, investigative concerns arise in litigation support. The accountant must ensure that a proper foundation exists for the basis of the calculation of future lost profits; that all assumptions incorporated into the work product are recognized and identified; that he or she understands where the expertise of the forensic accountant ends and the expertise of another starts; and that the issue of mitigation of damages is considered.

5.2.2 Investigative Mentality

The forensic accountant develops with his or her accounting knowledge an investigative mentality which allows the accountant to go beyond the bounds set out in either generally accepted accounting standards or auditing standards. For example:

1. Scope is not restricted as a result of materiality. Quite often, especially in the early stages of a management/employee fraud, the transactions are small and accordingly are more easily conveyed to the court to show a pattern of conduct that is deceitful. As the dollar value of the transactions and their complexity increase, the ability to convey the essence of the transaction is hampered and the forensic accountant's task is made more difficult.

2. The use of sampling is for the most part not acceptable in establishing evidence.

3. The more important difference affecting scope is the critical principle of the assumption of integrity of management and documentation especially in corporate investigation and white collar crime matters.

The investigative mentality develops in the search for best evidence. In a recent case of secret commissions involving a purchasing agent for a large retail distributor and a major vendor, it was determined that the vendor was selling product to the purchasing agent's company through a numbered company owned by their respective wives. At the time there was some concern as to how the plaintiff could overcome the documented evidence that placed ownership and control of the company with the wives. Bearing in mind the alternative sources of information, the working papers of the accountant for the company were obtained, and an organization description confirmed the shareholders as the wives but the executive decision makers as the husbands. Thus the best evidence no longer made it necessary for one to imply that notwithstanding ownership, control had to rest with the husbands.

Through the course of seeking evidence and information the forensic accountant will become involved in the interviewing process. This process by itself is another art to master. One of the possibilities for which the forensic accountant must be prepared is the question of how to properly handle a confession in such a way that the evidence is admissible.

The investigative mentality is best developed by one's continued experience in the witness box. It is through this process that the forensic accountant's eyes are opened, because counsel for the other side raises issues and possibilities that may not have formed a part of the accountant's consideration, assessment, and interpretation of the evidence to that point in time. Repeated involvement as a forensic witness creates a greater awareness of what is relevant and must be considered, such that the witness can present financial evidence in an independent and objective manner to reflect the reality of the situation.

5.3 REFLECTIONS ON FORENSIC ACCOUNTING BY FORENSIC ACCOUNTANTS

When the author circulated a questionnaire among the staff members of Peat Marwick Lindquist Holmes, a Toronto-based firm of chartered accountants responsible for the forensic and investigative accounting practice, response. were quite insightful and should be of interest to the reader.

Q.1. *How would you distinguish forensic accounting, fraud auditing, and investigative auditing from financial auditing?*

A. The distinction is related to the goals one is trying to achieve. Financial auditing attempts to enable the rendering of an opinion by the auditor as to whether a set of transactions is fairly presented in terms of Generally Accepted Accounting Principles. The financial statements upon which the opinion is rendered are always the representations of management. The auditor is primarily concerned with quantum (hence the concept of materiality comes into play), and generally is not concerned about whether or not the financial statements communicate the policies, intentions, or goals of management.

Forensic accounting, fraud auditing, and investigative auditing measure financial transactions in relation to various other authorities (e.g., the Criminal Code, an insurance contract, institutional policies or other guidelines for conduct or reporting). The report is prepared by the accountant/auditor rather than by the client or subject, and does not necessarily include the rendering of an opinion on the findings. In the investigation, one does not reject evidence as being "immaterial"—indeed, the smallest item can be the largest clue to the truth of the matter. Finally, whereas quantum is obviously an issue, even more important is the determination of the context—the mind and intentions of the criminal, the integrity of an insurance "accident," or the reasons for a particular occurrence.

However, in one important respect, these different practices must be identical. That is, the auditor/accountant must be skilled, experienced, and must maintain his or her independence and objectivity.

B. Forensic accounting is a general term used to describe any investigation of a financial nature that can result in some matter that has legal consequence.

Fraud auditing is a specialized discipline within forensic accounting, which involves the investigation of a particular criminal activity, namely fraud.

Investigative auditing involves the review of financial documentation for a specific purpose, which could relate to litigation support and insurance claims as well as criminal matters.

The objective of financial auditing is to provide the auditor with a degree o assurance in giving an opinion with respect to a company's financial statements. The materiality level of an investigative auditing engagement is much lower and more focused than that of the normal financial auditing engagement.

Q.2. *How would you define what you do as a forensic accountant?*

A. I think of myself as one who seeks out the truth.

B. I would define my forensic accounting responsibilities as follows:

> Investigation and analysis of financial documentation
>
> Communication of the findings from my investigation in the form of a report, accounting schedules, and document briefs
>
> Coordination of and assistance in further investigation, including the possibility of appearing in court as an expert witness

C. My role is that of an objective observer or expert. The final report that is issued as a result of my work will be used to negotiate some sort of settlement, be it financial or be it imprisonment. My role as a forensic accountant extends beyond the particular financial circumstances and seems to be one of an objective individual who provides the buffer between, in civil instances, the client and counsel, and in criminal instances, the investigator and Crown. Therefore, I am considered an integral member of the team of professionals assigned to any given case.

Related to the specific work that I do, it has been described to me, and I agree, that the makeup of a given forensic accountant is one-third businessman, one-third investigator, and one-third accountant.

Q.3. *What qualities of mind and/or body should a forensic accountant possess?*

A. Creativity—The ability to step out of what would otherwise be a normal business situation and consider alternative interpretations that might not necessarily make business sense

Curiosity—The desire to find out what has taken place in a given set of circumstances

Perseverance—The ability to push forward even when the circumstances either don't appear to substantiate the particular instance being investigated or when the documentation is very onerous and is a needle-in-a-haystack scenario

Common sense—Keeping a "real world" perspective

Businessman—To understand how businesses actually operate, not how business transactions are recorded

Confidence—To believe both in yourself and in your findings so that you can persevere when faced with cross-examination

B. As with any other pursuit, a healthy mind in a healthy body is a solid foundation. Beyond that, one should have generous proportions of common sense, inquisitiveness, skepticism, and an ability to avoid the natural tendency to prejudice (i.e., fairness and independence).

In addition, because forensic work can lead ultimately to court appearances, good posture, grooming, vocal projection, and stamina can all be valuable attributes.

C. The foremost quality of mind and/or body required of a forensic accountant is independence. An independent mind is required because a forensic accountant is often forced to balance conflicting opinions about the same piece of documentation.

The second major quality would be an intense sense of curiosity coupled with a sense of order (i.e., a desire to put the puzzle back together).

D. Common Sense/street smarts

Sensitive/understanding of human behavior

Analytical/logical/clear

Able to simplify complexities and delete jargon

Not prone to lose forest for the trees

Able to identify and assess alternative explanations and interpretations

Can quickly assess cost-benefit of pursuing alternative avenues of investigation and reporting contents/formats.

E. The forensic accountant needs to be calm, cool, and collected. The forensic accountant must possess good business judgment, and also have a mind that can deal with esoteric issues. Must also have a mind that can deal with precise matters in a very logical way.

A forensic accountant involved in litigation needs to be physically fit to withstand the long days and long nights of investigation, and preparation for and attendance at trial. The forensic accountant needs to have a pleasant appearance and demeanor so that he will not be offensive when in the witness box.

Q.4. *What skills are most important to the successful practice of forensic accounting?*

A. Solid technical accounting and financial skills—the basis of your "expertise"

Ability to quickly prioritize issues and map out a "game plan"—good judgment

Ability to communicate well—both verbally and in writing—is necessary to obtaining information, directing your staff, presenting your findings, and achieving your desired results. Even the best-planned and executed assignment can fail if you are unable to clearly and concisely present your findings

B. A forensic accountant needs to be precise, pay attention to detail, and be a broad thinker, that is, not suffer from tunnel vision.

C. When looking at a given forensic accounting engagement, there are two major areas that come to mind in the completion of a given case. First, there is the investigative aspect, and second, there is the communication aspect. I feel that investigative skills would include areas such as the ability to assimilate large volumes of information, general organization and administrative skills, use of the microcomputer or an understanding of the abilities of the microcomputer and interpersonal skills. Communication skills would include the ability to write a comprehensive report in an understandable fashion.

D. Communications skills: oral/written

Interpersonal skills

Listening skills

Ability to synthesize/integrate

Ability to identify/prioritize objectives/issues

6

FORENSIC AND INVESTIGATIVE ACCOUNTING: A CASE APPROACH

Accountants and auditors can develop fraud awareness and the investigative mentality through a case study approach. A brief review of the potential for white-collar crime within the accounting system is followed by case studies, first, relating to the purchases, payables, and payment system; and second, to the sales, receivables, and receipts system. There are a variety of ways individuals might fraudulently steal or embezzle company assets:

1. Through the purchase, payables, and payment system (i.e., false expense reports, false supplier invoices, and other false information)
2. Through the sales, receivables, and receipts system (i.e., front-end fraud, lapping, and false sales invoices)

But such fraud, theft, and embezzlement can be proven by uncovering evidence that establishes:

1. The job role of the accused within the accounting system
2. The control exercised by the accused on the accounting system
3. The knowledge by the accused of the accounting system
4. The systematic pattern used in covering up the fraud
5. The extent of the fraud
6. The personal financial position of the accused, which can be relevant to motive and can illustrate benefit

To establish credibility and to prove the case beyond a reasonable doubt, it is wise to give the benefit of the doubt to the accused. When establishing the situations and the extent of the fraud, pick only those examples or specific items of theft, fraud, or embezzlement that are unassailable.

It is often essential in crimes against a business to obtain evidence from company employees and those who had access to the assets that were allegedly misappropriated. It has to be established for each and every person who had access that he or she did not take the assets in question.

6.1 FRAUD WITHIN THE PURCHASES, PAYABLES, AND PAYMENTS SYSTEM

The purchases, payables, and payments system is the accounting system that records and controls a company's acquisition of assets and its incurrence of expenses. It records, for example, the purchase of fixed assets and inventory and the payment of salaries and sales-promotion expenses. False entries in books and supporting documents for purchases and payments can be used to perpetrate a fraud on a company. The main attack falls into three categories:

1. False expense reports
2. False supplier invoices
3. False information

6.1.1 False Expense Reports

Expense reports prepared and submitted for payment or reimbursement to the company are false if they contain:

1. Nonbusiness items
2. Inflated items
3. Fictitious items
4. Duplicate items

A company credit card can be used for personal items. If the entire amount of the account is paid and expensed by the company, then a fraud may be occurring.

The issues are as follows:

1. Is the expense item an allowable business-related expense?
2. Is the expense amount the actual amount incurred?
3. Is the expense ultimately charged to the business? If yes, is there evidence of any reimbursement by the employee?

To address the first issue, it is necessary to determine the company's policy regarding allowable business expenses. To address the second issue, it is necessary to obtain the supplier's copies of the original expense vouchers and compare them with those submitted in support of the expense report. It is also necessary to understand the approval-and-payment system in effect. Who approved the expense reports? How were the expense reports categorized in the accounting records? Were they adjusted through a journal entry at a later date to reflect their personal nature? Was there any pattern in the submission, approval, and/or recording of the fraudulent expense reports?

6.1.2 False Supplier Invoices

Suppliers invoices prepared and submitted for payment to the company are false if:

1. No goods have been delivered or services rendered
2. The quantity or price is inflated
3. The quality has been compromised

The delivery of goods or services to a location other than a business location (for the use and benefit of the perpetrator) is a common technique, as is the payment to a "friendly" supplier when no goods or services were actually provided. Payments of inflated amounts to suppliers often reflect the existence of secret commissions (bribes).

The issues to be addressed by the investigative accountant are as follows:

1. Were the goods and services actually provided?

2. Did the company receive the benefit?

3. What was the approval-and-payment system?

It is necessary to find out first whether the supplier company actually exists and next whether such goods or services were in fact provided. If they were provided, one must determine for whom.

It is often necessary to obtain the bills of lading, that is, the freight companies proof-of-delivery slips, to confirm the location where goods and services were delivered.

As with false expense reports, one must understand the approval-and-payment system.

6.1.3 False Information

A business receives vast amounts of information, and subject to the existing systems of internal control, relies upon it in making decisions and in initiating, executing, and recording transactions. If this information is false, a business can be deceived, resulting in deprivation and hence placing the company at economic risk.

Examples of false information that businesses may rely upon include:

1. False financial statements

2. Overstated accounts receivable listings

3. Overstated statements of income and net worth

4. False general journal entries

5. Altered internal company records

6. Fictitious customer credit information

7. False asset valuations.

Some of the issues to be addressed are as follows:

1. Is the summary information presented (accounts receivable listing, financial statements) consistent with the underlying books and records?

2. Are the entries in the general journal properly approved? Are they appropriate and consistent with the facts?

3. Can transactions be confirmed with third parties?

To address the first issue it is necessary to determine the representation made by the person or company under investigation and the understanding reached. Once this has been done, the books and records supporting the summary financial information in question can be examined from the appropriate perspective.

To address the other issues, it is necessary to understand the accounting systems in effect. It is important to contact third parties to review and discuss their books and records, and then to compare that information with the information represented to the victim.

6.2 FRAUD WITHIN THE SALES RECEIVABLE RECEIPTS SYSTEM

This part of the accounting system records the company's sales and revenue collections. Various fraudulent activities can occur with this system, primarily in three categories:

1. Front-end fraud
2. False sales invoices
3. Lapping

6.2.1 Front-End Fraud

Company revenue may be diverted before it ever reaches the sales, receivables, and receipts system, thus circumventing the accounting system entirely. This is commonly called a *front-end fraud*. A front-end fraud occurs when company products are sold for cash, the sale and the receipt of cash are not recorded, and the cash is diverted—usually directly into the pocket of the perpetrator. A front-end fraud occurs when a company's customers are improperly directed to take their business elsewhere, thus depriving the company of business and profits it could otherwise have earned. A front-end fraud occurs when special or unusual revenues and cost reductions, such as purchase rebates, are received and misappropriated. The issues to be addressed in front-end fraud are:

1. Do recorded sales represent all company sales?

2. Has the company unexpectedly experienced reduced sales from some its oldest and best customers?

3. Are all revenues recorded?

Generally front-end fraud is characterized by management override internal controls. In the situation in which no sales have been recorded, there is nothing in the sales accounting system to red-flag an unpaid or overdu account. As a result, unrecorded sales are difficult to detect. However, actua inventory on hand has been depleted. If the company has a good inventor accounting system, the unrecorded sale may be detected.

Service businesses such as a ferry service and the theater and movi business operate primarily with cash sales and have no inventory systems Front-end fraud in these types of businesses is extremely difficult to detect

Benefit may be established through a review of personal bank accounts i they reveal unexplained cash deposits. Otherwise the net worth approach may be necessary to establish benefit.

The sales records and other supporting documents of both the victim and the customers (assuming they can be identified) should be analyzed for the period before the occurrence date of the alleged front-end fraud to determine business in the normal course.

6.2.2 False Sales Invoices

A company sales invoice can be altered to show a lower sale amount than was actually the case. The difference between the real sale amount and the adjusted lower amount can then be misappropriated without the accounting system showing a red flag.

Questions to ask include:

1. Are recorded sale amounts the actual sales amounts?

2. Can sales be confirmed with customers?

3. Are sale amounts reasonable in the circumstances?

It is important to obtain and examine all original copies of an invoice and all the related books of original entry. Again, the investigator must become familiar with the accounting system and understand the person's position within the system. Did the person have the necessary authority to perpetrate this crime? Did the person have the opportunity?

6.2.3 Lapping

When cash receipts from customer A are misappropriated and the misappropriation is subsequently covered up by recording the receipt of monies from customer B to the credit of customer A (to the extent of the earlier misappropriation), lapping is occurring.

Appropriate questions include:

1. Are the amounts recorded as owing to the company actually still owing to the company?
2. Are deposits from Peter being used to cover Paul's debts?

To deal with these issues it is necessary to understand the system in effect for receiving customer payments, making bank deposits, and preparing entries to customer accounts.

Who first received the payments? Who prepared the company bank deposit? Who updated the customer accounts? Have any accounts been written off? Who approved the write-off? It is also often necessary to contact customers and obtain their records of payments, including paid checks and remittance advices. Do their records show payment of specific invoices that are shown as unpaid in the victim company's records?

6.3 MANAGEMENT FRAUD WITHIN THE PURCHASES, PAYABLES, AND PAYMENTS SYSTEM

6.3.1 Regina v. Lipsome

This case is an example of management (president) exercising influence over its suppliers to obtain a secret commission. The deceitful document was the supplier's invoice bearing the name "Fashion Coordinators, Inc." The supplier's billing to the customer was inflated by the amount of the secret commission paid to the president.

The customer, an agent for a major retail department store, purchased th goods from suppliers in foreign countries. The president took an activ interest by personally participating in arranging contracts between foreig suppliers and the company. The foreign suppliers realized that contract could be obtained only because they agreed to pay to the president's persona bank account in a foreign jurisdiction an amount equal to two percent of th value of the business to be transacted with their new customer. This additiona fee, included as a cost of the product, was billed to the customer. In order t ensure that the higher cost would not be detected or questioned by anyone ir the purchasing department, the president approved all of these invoices fo payment.

One day the foreign supplier, confident that he could retain the company' business, informed a director of this arrangement. In the end both parties lost.

The fact that the president was performing a clerical function (i.e., review of suppliers' invoices for approval of payment) was an indication of the activity. In any investigation, departures from a normal business practice should be questioned.

6.3.2 Regina v. Barter

Don Barter entered into an agreement with Norgard to start a construction business. It was agreed that Norgard would finance the business and Barter would manage and operate the business, to be known as Norgard Construction. Barter agreed to accept a salary plus expenses and to share the profits of the business equally with Norgard. The business mainly consisted of constructing service stations. The operation progressed and the business showed a profit for the first three years of operation.

Norgard did not take an active part in the construction business. He continued to operate his own plastering company. The new business, Norgard Construction, was to operate as a division of his company, P.L.R. Plastering Limited. Norgard, the sole check-signing officer and absentee-owner, would visit the office regularly to sign checks, some of which were blank.

Barter tendered and obtained contracts, hired subcontractors, hired and fired employees, and purchased goods necessary to operate the business without interference or direction from Norgard. Barter could also purchase material he required through the construction business and charge this amount to himself on the business books as a form of salary.

Norgard was aware that over the years Barter had erected a barn on his farm and renovated other buildings, including his residence. Barter informed Norgard that he had obtained a grant from the government for $100,000 to finance the renovations and improvements.

Gradually Norgard Construction began to have difficulty paying its suppliers and was eventually petitioned into bankruptcy by a creditor. The company's debts exceeded $100,000 at this time. Barter gave no explanation for the shortage of funds except to say that he had miscalculated the actual cost of the various construction jobs. An examination of the books of account, canceled checks, and available supporting documentation revealed that Barter had defrauded Norgard Construction of $287,000 by various means.

As general manager of Norgard Construction Company, Barter was responsible for the day-to-day operations. The owner was usually absent and the general manager was afforded a degree of trust. At the same time the absentee owner retained signing authority over all checks and control over all policy decisions.

In his private capacity as a farmer, Barter incurred debts with suppliers who also dealt with him as general manager of Norgard. Barter personally owed one of these suppliers, United Cooperatives of Ontario, more than $9,800. In June 1970, Barter purchased a $4.30 item, documented by invoice #512403 from the supplier and made out in pencil. Later the penciled information on this invoice was erased. Information was typed in, indicating instead that the company, Norgard, had purchased $3,500 worth of material for a job then in progress. On the strength of this typed document, the absentee owner signed a check for $3,500 to the supplier believing, of course, that the disbursement was to the benefit of the company. When the supplier received the check, he credited Barter's *personal* account, reducing the debt to $6,300 on Barter's instruction. (Exhibits 6.1 and 6.2).

The alteration of documents (erasures and/or information stroked out) is at times the only indication of fraudulent activity. It discloses the state of mind (intent) of the person making the entry. Such alterations frequently occur in the earlier stages of a fraud when the perpetrator has yet to perfect the scheme.

In another example, G&M Forest Products invoiced Norgard for the sale of "Roof Trusses" with delivery scheduled for a construction site. However, the back of the invoice disclosed a notation that described the route to Barter's farm. The building of his barn required roof trusses. A review of the bill of lading confirmed the redirection.

UNITED CO-OPERATIVES OF ONTARIO
UCO

BRANCH _____

NAME _Don Barton_   DATE _July 9,_ 19_70_

ADDRESS _____

TERMS CODE	CASH SALE	CHARGE	REC'D. ON ACCT.	CREDIT ACCT.	INITIAL
QUANTITY	DESCRIPTION			PRICE	AMOUNT
100	Cobalt salt				2.40
100	Common fine salt				1.90
					4.30
	Received by _Barton_				
			TAX		

TERMS: ACCOUNT DUE 20 DAYS AFTER MONTHLY STATEMENT.
1½% PER MONTH SERVICE CHARGE ON PAST DUE ACCOUNTS.

TOTAL $ 4.30

512403

I HEREBY CERTIFY THAT THE GOODS ARE PURCHASED FOR FARM USE _____

EXHIBIT 6.1. United Co-Operatives of Ontario invoice.

UNITED CO-OPERATIVES OF ONTARIO
<u>UCO</u>

Uxbridge, Ont.
_____
BRANCH

DATE ___May 30,___ 19_70_

NAME ___Norgard Construction Co.___

ADDRESS ___485 Kennedy Rd., Scarboro, Ont.___

TERMS CODE	CASH SALE	CHARGE ✓	REC'D. ON ACCT.	CREDIT ACCT.	INITIAL
QUANTITY	DESCRIPTION			PRICE	AMOUNT
	For the supply of steel posts				
	and farm type fence for the				
	Gulf Oil. Belleville, Ont.				$3,500.00
					TAX
					TOTAL

_6204   9494_

CD June/70

TERMS: ACCOUNT DUE 20 DAYS AFTER MONTHLY STATEMENT.
1½% PER MONTH SERVICE CHARGE ON PAST DUE ACCOUNTS.

512403

I HEREBY CERTIFY THAT THE GOODS ARE PURCHASED FOR FARM USE ....

EXHIBIT 6.2. United Co-Operatives of Ontario invoice. From a study of Norgard documents, one becomes familiar with Norgard's typewriter. In this case it bears a

These two major proofs went a long way toward convincing the trial judge of Barter's guilt.

6.4 EMPLOYEE FRAUD WITHIN THE PURCHASES, PAYABLES, AND PAYMENTS SYSTEM

6.4.1 Regina v. Down and Out

It is obvious that most perpetrators of illegal activity wish to remain hidden and anonymous. If they own companies engaging in illegal activities they will wish to, and indeed strive to, remain in the background. They may wish to create official records showing that someone else owns the business and making them appear as the directing mind.

It is often useful for a perpetrator to geographically separate his corporate activities from one other (if he has several companies) and from his home turf. This may in part be due to a belief that an investigator will have to expend significantly more energy to identify the true owner. Others may believe that appointing their lawyer as the nominal owner will protect disclosure.

Within a corporate setting employees will attempt to hide their ownership in another company that is doing business with or stealing customers from their employer. This results in the employee taking for his or her own benefit a rake-off or commission from the employer.

The main focus of an investigation into suspected hidden ownership is directed to identify the directing mind of the company. Who has authority? Who appears to report to whom? Who received information, particularly financial information? Who signs legal documents or banking agreements? Do suspected owners receive commissions, bonuses, or loan advances? In *Regina v. Down and Out* the chief purchasing agent for a municipality and the town engineer together set up a phony supplier company. The dummy company, Sparks Engineering and Drafting Supply, was ostensibly providing the town with certain office supplies, to the tune of some $320,000, from 1975 to 1982. In fact no supplies were ever delivered.

The fraud surfaced when two accounts payable clerks began to wonder why they had never seen anyone from the vendor organization call on the town's purchasing agent. Sparks did not even send the town a Christmas card in spite of the amount of business ostensibly placed with it. Then one day one of the clerks decided to dial the telephone number printed on Spark's invoice. To her surprise an auto body shop in Toronto answered her call. She reported her concerns to Douglas Down. After this incident the clerk noticed the telephone number on Sparks' invoice had been changed. She called repeatedly. Each time she heard the following tape-recorded message, "Sorry, we're not in right now. Please phone back later." She discussed her concerns with the other clerk, who had also noticed some unusual things about Sparks; for example, the invoice had a post office address (Exhibit 6.3). She also noticed that all of the Sparks invoices were for amounts under $500 (the town had a policy that all orders for goods in excess of $500 had to be put out for bid), and that checks issued in payment for Sparks invoices were always under $2,000 (the town's policy was that checks issued in amounts over $2,000 were to be approved by the town treasurer, who signed the checks by hand). Checks under $2,000 were signed by a check-signing machine after being approved by Douglas Down.

One clerk also noted that Douglas Down insisted on delivering the checks to Sparks himself, rather than having them mailed as were all other suppliers checks. Nor were checks for Sparks ever issued when Douglas Down was on vacation. And most of Sparks purchases were ordered for the town engineering department by Richard Out.

The clerks then reported their concerns to the town treasurer. He talked to the receiver in the warehouse, who informed him that to the best of his recollection no Sparks truck had ever delivered goods.

Then Richard Out was interviewed. He admitted he and Douglas Down had set up Sparks to defraud the town.

The investigative accountant retained in the case performed the following tasks:

1. Prepared a listing of invoices rendered by Sparks and paid by the town
2. Analyzed the activity in the bank account maintained by Sparks to help determine whether Sparks was carrying on business in the normal course
3. Analyzed the activity in the personal bank accounts maintained by the two accused to assist in identifying financial benefit
4. Prepared a schedule setting out Sparks' purchases from suppliers and subsequent resale at the 20 percent markup to the town to quantify the amount of the alleged abuse

SPARKS Equipment Service & Drafting Supplies

P.O. BOX 2704, STATION 'F'
SCARBOROUGH, ONTARIO, M1W 3P3
416-498-5237

Sold To:

Town of Markham
8911 Woodbine Ave.
Markham, Ontario
L3R 1A1

INVOICE NO. 3749
DATE Oct. 13.1982

QUANTITY	DESCRIPTION	PRICE	AMOUNT
2 doz.	Black 3–Ring Binders	$12.95	$310.80 ✓
	Less 5% Discount		15.54 ✓
			$295.26 ✓
	Prov. Tax 7%		20.67 ✓
	Total		$315.93 ✓
			======

SUPPLIER #

VOUCHER # 123548

DATE Oct. 13/82   AMOUNT 315.93

INVOICE # 3749   P.O. #   LOT. PURCH. REQ.

ACCOUNT # 0300   0300   00001   0

PRICES CHECKED ✓   EXTENSION CHECKED ✓   BATCH

DEPARTMENT HEAD APPROVED   WEEK

EXHIBIT 6.3. Sparks invoice to municipality.

The analysis of the bank account records maintained on behalf of Sparks indicated that the only source of company funds were the checks received from the town. The only uses of funds were checks issued to Out and to Out's friend, and during the last few months to Down. There were no disbursements for such items as purchases from suppliers, for payroll, for overhead, or for other normal business expenses.

The analysis of the activity in the personal bank accounts maintained by Out indicated that Out's income was heavily augmented by amounts transferred from Sparks. It also revealed many checks issued to Down and many checks written to cash. The analysis of Down's bank accounts also indicated that large amounts had been deposited in excess of his known sources of income.

Out was confronted with this information. He admitted that Sparks had not delivered any supplies to the town, but had simply rendered invoices that were duly paid. He also admitted that the profits were split, with 45 percent going to Down and the remainder to himself.

6.5 VENDOR FRAUD WITHIN THE PURCHASES, PAYABLES, AND PAYMENTS SYSTEM

Another of the more common frauds involves scams perpetrated against a company by its vendors, contractors, and suppliers. These frauds are even more difficult to detect during a financial audit than those committed by management. The outsider often has an inside confederate who steers him clear of control-system snags, or "greases" the way. That combination is really hard to beat so long as the co-conspirators do not have a falling out.

But sometimes ingenious vendors perpetrate frauds by themselves with no help from insiders.

6.5.1 Regina v. Kotowski

Kotowski, president of Central Fuel Company Limited, defrauded a school district by charging it for fuel that had not, in fact, been delivered to a high school in Fort Frances, Ontario.

For three years Central Fuel Company submitted the lowest bid to the school board for the delivery of fuel oil to the school, even though one of the other bidders was a major oil company, the same company that supplied fuel oil to Central Fuel Company for its sale to the school. Since Central Fuel offered the lowest price per gallon (14.5 cents) the school board accepted its bid. It was later established that the company was able to charge the lower market price per gallon because it billed the school board for oil that had not in fact, been supplied. The meter on the company's oil truck was rigged to continue running after the oil was shut off. The gallons of fuel oil ostensibly delivered were subsequently billed to the school district.

Before the documentary evidence could be collected the premises of the Central Fuel Company were destroyed by fire. Since the documents required to complete the fraud investigation were no longer available, the forensic accountants had to seek documentation from various third parties.

The sales invoices submitted by Central Fuel Company were available from the school board's Department of Supply and Services, as were their canceled checks and their agreement with Central Fuel Company. Documents concerning Central Fuel Company's supply of oil were obtained from the major oil company. Their invoices to Central Fuel and their statements of account, indicating the payments received from Central Fuel for the purchase of the oil, were reviewed. From this information schedules were prepared to show the total number of gallons invoiced and the invoiced dollar amount of those gallons for each of the three school years. This information, however, was useless without evidence by an engineer who could calculate what the high school heating system should have consumed in terms of gallons of oil. The engineer analyzed the capacity of that system by determining the number of heating degree days during each of the school years, making an extremely conservative assumption that the doors and windows of the school were open all winter long. The number of gallons of oil required by the school according to the engineer was much lower than the number of gallons invoiced by Central Fuel to the school for each of the three years. Color graphs were prepared for each of the three years to show the contrast between gallons invoiced versus the expert engineer's assessments. These visual aids enabled the court to readily grasp the meaning of the financial data presented in evidence. (See Exhibit 6.4). In order to further support the evidence of the engineer, the forensic accountants produced a schedule to show the number of gallons delivered in the year following Kotowski's dismissal (See Exhibit 6.5) It was less than the engineer's assessment.

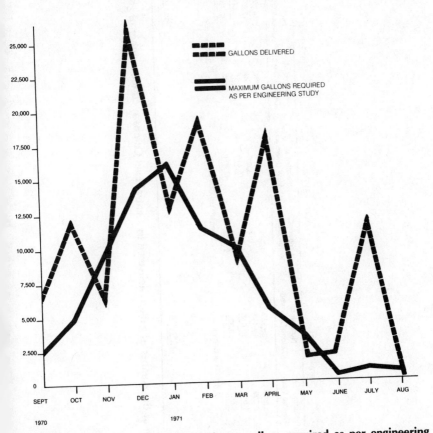

EXHIBIT 6.4. Gallons delivered—maximum gallons required as per engineering study.

	1969—1970		1970—1971		1971—1972		1972—1973	
	Number of Degree Days	Number of Gallons Delivered	Number of Degree Days	Number of Gallons Delivered	Number of Degree Days	Number of Gallons Delivered	Number of Degree Days	Number of Gallons Delivered
December	1,561	12,916	1,908	26,959	1,745	18,883	1,893	14,691
January	2,106	25,555	2,239	12,447	2,195	9,953	1,720	11,467
February	1,694	18,595	1,550	18,618	1,848	18,475	1,561	6,000
	5,361	57,066	5,697	58,024	5,788	47,311	5,174	32,158
Deliveries by:	Central Fuel Company		Central Fuel Company		Central Fuel Company		Gulf Canada	
Maximum Number of Gallons required per Engineering Dept.		38,599		41,018		41,674		37,253

EXHIBIT 6.5. Central Fuel Company. Comparison of the number of gallons delivered by Central Fuel Company to the number of gallons delivered by Gulf Canada.

6.6 MANAGEMENT FRAUD WITHIN THE SALES RECEIVABLE RECEIPTS SYSTEM

6.6.1 United States v. Goldblum, Levin, Lewis et al.

This case involves the Equity Funding Insurance Company of America and was popularized in the videotape, "The Billion Dollar Bubble."

On January 1, 1978 the shares of Equity Funding Corporation of America were trading on the New York Stock Exchange in moderate volume at about $37. Three months later, on March 28, trading in Equity Funding shares was stopped by the SEC after a week of fevered activity had reduced their price to $14.

In spite of its spectacular growth and earnings history, Equity Funding had not actually earned a penny of profit in the preceding four years—it had lost money. The fraud was not a sophisticated computer operation run by a small group, as was first suspected. Instead a large number of employees had systematically developed and maintained a completely false picture of sustained growth and prosperity that pervaded the company's operations. Using the inflated values of the shares of the company, they were able to acquire a small empire of other companies with real assets. As one method of extending the fraud outlived its usefulness, the conspirators turned to another.

Art Lewis, the chief actuary, had access to the computer facilities and was also responsible for preparing the annual financial statements of the corporation. In 1969 the preparation of the financial statements was delayed. Necessary information was not available from the computer facility, primarily because certain computer programs had not been completely debugged. As a result the executive vice-president, Fred Levin, suggested a net income figure be picked and the sales estimated using this number.

It was discovered soon after that the actual results were far short of the reported (and estimated) results. Art Lewis and Fred Levin took steps to create false insurance policies to inflate actual revenues and profit to the levels of those reported. This maintained the stock price of the corporation on the market. These policies were entered onto the computer as "99" policies so they could subsequently be identified. In addition, if a request was received from an auditor to confirm a policy, the "99" policies were automatically excluded from being selected for confirmation by the computer. At this time, Levin and Lewis considered their actions to be a temporary expedient in order to maintain the company's stock in the market.

Unfortunately, because this revenue was fictitious there was not corresponding cash flow to the company, and the company soon experienced cash shortages. Stanley Goldblum, the president, asked Levin and Lewis to obtain cash in order to subsidize the insurance and other operations related to the corporation.

This necessitated selling the false insurance policies to insurance underwriters for approximately twice the annual premium. The phony policies were being sold to the underwriters and cash was coming into Equity Funding Insurance Company. What Levin and Lewis did not consider at the time was that, after the initial payment on the insurance policy to the underwriter Equity Funding would have to make the yearly payments for the fictitiou insured persons. (Eventually they even began to "kill" the fake insured bodie in order to collect real proceeds.)

The payments on the fictitious policies caused an even worse cash flow problem and necessitated the creation of even more fictitious policies an their sale to the insurance underwriters. At one point they calculated that b the end of 10 years they would have sold more insurance policies than ther were citizens in the United States.

Astonishingly, with dozens of people intimately acquainted with the detai of the fraud and with audited financial statements, the secret was kept for decade. Only when Equity Funding fired the "wrong" employee, Ron Secris did the story begin to unfold. Publicly the stock price plunged. Huge bloc changed hands at the last minute, resulting in an endless series of lawsuits buyers and sellers tried to conclude or renege on transactions. Eventually employees and three auditors were indicted for fraud. The fraud had grown a few short years to the following proportions:

1. Assets were overstated by over $100,000,000
2. Fictitious funded loans to policyholders totaled $62.3 million
3. Fictitious bonds totaled $24.6 million
4. Fictitious commercial paper totaled $8 million
5. In 1972 Equity Funding listed assets of $737.5 million and a net wort $143.4 million
6. The subsequent investigation and audit showed actual assets to worth only $488.9 million and actual net worth was negative $42 milli
7. Over 200 people (insiders) were aware of some aspect of the fraud be its exposure.

8. Thousands of fictitious insurance policies were generated by company computers.

9. Stock certificates were counterfeited in the company's own print shop.

6.7 EMPLOYEE FRAUD WITHIN THE SALES RECEIVABLE RECEIPTS SYSTEM

6.7.1 Regina v. Harvey

Smith Transport Company operated a trucking terminal in Belleville, Ontario. Their accounts receivable clerk, Harvey, had been a loyal and faithful employee for over eight years. The terminal manager often complimented her for the effort she put into the business, evidenced by the amount of work she frequently took home.

Harvey began part-time employment with Smith Transport, Belleville Terminal, as a rating and billing division office clerk. She later took over as accounts receivable clerk and appeared to digest the instructions easily, showing a keen interest. She was able to train new rate clerks and billers and answer all rate requests from customers through the day.

Harvey soon learned to handle compensation reports, refund or overcharge claims, interline accounts payable, intermediate terminals procedure, terminals engineering reports, and payroll work, and was able to replace any member of the office staff while they were on vacation. She appeared to be well liked by the office personnel, drivers, and customers, and seemed to be a real asset to the company.

Harvey's main function each day was to balance the cash received with the sales invoices and prepare a cash deposit for the bank and a cash report for processing in the computer. She would process all incoming checks from charge account customers by matching checks to the applicable invoice copies and preparing a deposit for the bank and a receivable report for processing in the computer. She would present the cash and receivable reports to the manager for his signature, along with the customer checks and cash.

The supporting sales invoices were always in sealed and stapled envelopes for each report. The envelopes were not opened and verified by the manager. If the total of the bank deposit agreed with the total of the sales invoices, he would sign the report.

Harvey would work on the Accounts Receivable Aged Analysis, a listing of all outstanding pro-bills prepared in Toronto; she questioned certain delinquent accounts for payment. She often took the analysis home because she said she was too busy to do it during the day.

The manager looked at the Accounts Receivable Aged Analysis monthly and questioned certain delinquent customer accounts. Harvey informed the manager of checks arriving after her contact with the delinquent customer. She advised her manager that a major customer had had serious problems converting to a computer accounting system, and as a result, requested that Smith Transport be patient with the amount of old outstanding receivables.

Harvey became ill; her house was listed for sale. Smith Transport decided to hire a new person to replace Harvey.

The new person began the collection work on the two largest charge account customers because successful collection of these accounts would immediately reduce the 60- and 90-day totals on the Accounts Receivable Aged analysis.

The first major customer was asked if they were having computer problems, and the response was negative. The manager was advised that the receivables had in fact been paid. When Smith Transport checked their deposit slips and reports, they found checks from their major customer deposited and applied to older sales invoices and to other customer sales invoices and not to the specific sales invoices submitted by the customer with the check.

Through investigation it was determined that the accounts receivable clerk had conducted a lapping scheme over a period of six years. The lap grew so large during this period that she had to take the aged receivable analysis home in the evenings, along with the paid and unpaid sales invoices, in order to set aside those invoices for payment during the next day to ensure a favorable aged receivable analysis in the following month. As the lap grew, the daily cash receipts were no longer sufficient to cover the previously misappropriated funds. Accordingly the clerk began to apply checks received from larger customers of the company to cover up the already-paid sales invoices of other customers.

In attempting to establish benefit to the accused, the known personal bank accounts of the accused and her husband were examined. An amount of $35,000 in cash was found deposited to these bank accounts over and above personal income during the relevant period (Exhibit 6.6). Had the manager examined any one deposit and report, lapping could have been detected.

Total Deposits		$113,227.04
Less-known nonpayroll deposits:		
Family Allowance	$ 232.00	
Family Finance Plan Loan	23,103.14	
Transfer from A/C 1012	232.00	
Smith Transport Credit Union	1,049.35	
Bancardchek	920.00	
Tax Refund	217.57	
Not Sufficient Funds	2,906.42	
Loan	1,450.00	
Ontario Credit Union	1,000.00	
Miscellaneous	10.11	31,220.59
		82,106.45
Less-known payroll deposits:		
Richard Harvey payroll checks	29,570.08	
Lois Harvey payroll checks	8,971.73	38,541.81
Balance of deposits whose source unknown		$ 43,564.64
Composed of:		
Cash		$ 35,477.19
Checks		8,087.45
		$ 43,564.64

EXHIBIT 6.6. A statement of the apparent sources of deposits to the known bank account in the name of Richard and Lois Harvey.

6.8 CUSTOMER FRAUD WITHIN THE SALES RECEIVABLE RECEIPTS SYSTEM

Planned bankruptcy occurs when management has converted the assets of a business to its own benefit and then tries to conceal the conversion through formal bankruptcy proceedings. Characteristics include the following:

1. The business has established a reputation for trustworthiness in the business community

2. It sells tangible and highly salable products such as furniture

3. The business has little net worth

4. It has not been a financial success

5. A new person is introduced in a senior position

6. The business departs from its normal business practices with regard to purchasing, payments to suppliers, sales, and the granting of credit to customers

These changes in business conduct are likely to be followed by these manifestations:

1. The volume of inventory ordered from existing suppliers increases significantly. The suppliers will probably extend credit up to 60 days, largely as a result of their wish to retain the business and the established reputation of the company.

2. The unsuspecting suppliers will receive little or no payment. The scam will probably be completed within 60 days of the date of purchase of the inventory. After that time the suppliers are likely to become suspicious and might take action of some kind.

3. The company will refuse to sell its inventory on credit and sell only on COD basis. To get customers to pay cash, the selling price per unit may be at or below the company's cost as shown on supplier invoices.

4. If inventory remains on hand after the usual customers have been approached, it may be sold to new customers. Such sales tend to be non-arm's-length and are usually for cash. (Although the sales invoices may indicate the payment was made in cash, the deposit of the cash into the corporate bank account does not necessarily follow.)

5. If, after all these efforts to sell, inventory is still left at the site, it will be physically removed. The trail of the goods will be covered up to prevent detection.

A planned bankruptcy is designed, of course, to benefit those in control of the planned bankrupt. However, it is essential that no trail be left behind to enable the trustee in bankruptcy to retrieve the proceeds of the crime and return those proceeds to the bankrupt company. The techniques employed to block the path of the trustee are limited only by the perpetrator's imagination and will vary according to the circumstances.

6.8.1 Regina v. Rosen

This case illustrates the changes that took place in purchasing and payment activity just before the company bankruptcy. Brittany Antiques Limited was incorporated in October 1970. Rosen was the president of the company that sold antique furniture by auction and on a wholesale basis. For the fiscal year ended October 31, 1973, the company reported sales of $122,090, merchandise purchases of $90,265, and a net loss of $3,740.

In the fall of 1974 John Mac joined Rosen's firm. In January 1975 Brittany changed its buying habits to include large purchases of merchandise. Rosen and Mac went to the various furniture and gift shows in January and February 1975 in Toronto to become personally acquainted with the many dealers. They explained that they were in the business of buying and selling by auction, and mentioned they had a contract to supply furniture to two new motels in the Northern Ontario towns of North Bay and Kapuskasing.

In fact Brittany's new purchasing policy resulted in the acquisition of merchandise during the period of January 1975 to May 31, 1975, totaling $411,586.13. However, by June 24, 1975, Brittany's new payment policy resulted in only $10,248.86 being paid to these suppliers.

A key ingredient in a successfully planned bankruptcy is being able to blame someone for the failure of your corporation. Equally important, the transactions normally examined by the trustee in the search for corporate assets should not leave a trail of evidence—especially when it becomes apparent to the trustee that a large inventory discrepancy exists.

In May 1975 Brittany advertised the position "bookkeeper. . . chance for advancement to managerial position." The real Mr. John Peter Geslak, a Toronto accountant, called Brittany to apply for the position. He was advised by someone in Brittany's office to send in his resume. Because he was applying for several positions at this time, he had prepared several copies of his resume and simply sent one to Brittany. This was the last he heard from them about the position.

On April 9, 1975, Rosen went to see his bank manager to introduce a John Geslak as Brittany's new accountant. Rosen stated that Geslak would handle all of the firm's financial affairs and would have full signing authority for the firm (thus solving the problem of access to assets). A banking resolution was drawn up to this effect, and the authorized signature card was changed to show the name of John Peter Geslak.

With the changed policies, the new people, and an inventory of furniture boosted to its highest levels in the company's history, the planned bankruptcy was now ready for the next stage, the quick disposal. To document these activities the investigative accountant had to reconstruct the sales and cash receipts of Brittany.

Based on the available documentation, known sales of $245,222 occurred between April 15, 1975, and May 17, 1975. This amount included four invoices marked "paid in cash—John Geslak" dated April 28 and May 2, 12, and 15. But the bank records for Brittany did not disclose the deposit of *any* cash to the company's account.

Thus the introduction of a John Geslak into the operation of Brittany Antiques along with the sales invoices marked "paid in cash—John Geslak," enabled Rosen to claim that John Geslak must have taken this cash from the customer and, instead of depositing the cash in the company account, stole it.

This technique was employed to block the trustee's access to the furniture. It initially prevented the trustee from attacking Rosen because Rosen could blame his plight on the theft by his accountant John Geslak of the sale proceeds.

In a planned bankruptcy, time is of the essence. Most creditors will allow 30 to 60 days for payment, especially for more significant orders. They are, after all, in business to do business, and granting credit is an accepted practice and an accepted risk in business. With most of the purchases having occurred in March and April 1975, it was not surprising that in the latter part of May some of the suppliers would be pressuring Brittany for payment of account.

One of the better ways of buying time from Brittany's point of view was to issue checks to the suppliers. This was done commencing May 20, 1975. Checks totaling $65,285.33 were issued to 12 creditors between May 20 and May 26, 1975, when the bank balance as of May 20 was $1,209.20. Of course all of these checks were subsequently returned marked NSF (not sufficient funds).

On May 30, 1975, Rosen wrote to the suppliers saying, in part, "Our accountant has absconded with all deposits, placing our firm in a terrible position." (Exhibit 6.7)

On June 16, 1975, the landlord of Brittany's business premises had a bailiff lock the place for nonpayment of rent.

On July 15, 1975, Rosen filed an assignment request in bankruptcy for Brittany Antiques Limited.

BRITTANY ANTIQUE LTD.
AUCTION HOUSE

30 Baywood Rd. Unit 9
Rexdale, Ontario

Tel. 749-9791
749-9391

m9v 3z1

May 30, 1975

Dear Sir or Madame:

It is our sad misfortune to inform you at this time that for reasons beyond our control, our payment to you shall be somewhat delayed.
Our accountant has absconded with all deposits placing our firm in a terrible position. However, the police are presently looking for him and seem quite optimistic about his apprehension.
We have full intentions of meeting our obligations as soon as possible and beg your indulgence in this matter.

We remain very truly yours,

Brittany Antique Ltd.,

Carl Rosen
President

EXHIBIT 6.7. A further attempt by management to stall creditors from their accounts.

At the time of bankruptcy Rosen believed that the path of the trustee had been blocked, and with John Geslak having returned to his place of origin with the proceeds obtained by crime, it appeared initially that a planned bankruptcy had in fact succeeded.

However, when investigation commenced, it was determined that the real John F. Geslak in Toronto, Ontario, had had no relationship to Brittany Antiques Limited. The question then arose as to the real identity of the individual who had claimed to be John Geslak. Eventually investigation revealed that the accountant who had absconded with the firm's money was living in Hyannis, Massachusetts, after of course sharing the benefit with Rosen.

6.9 APPLICATIONS OF INVESTIGATIVE ACCOUNTING TO MURDER, ARSON, AND COMMERCIAL BRIBERY

6.9.1 Murder

Forensic accounting skills may be applied to homicide investigations for the following purposes: (1) to analyze and determine a possible financial motive for murder, (2) to analyze financial documentation relating to a murder for possible investigative leads, and (3) to identify possible payments on a contract for murder.

In determining financial motive the accounting analysis is directed primarily toward establishing any financial benefit to the accused as a result of that person's association with the murder victim. Benefit may be shown in various ways:

1. Payments by the victim to the accused (extortion)
2. Assets such as stocks, bonds, real estate, or collectibles transferred to the accused before or after the murder
3. Insurance proceeds paid to the accused as beneficiary under a policy
4. Other benefits, such as obtaining an interest in a business

When analyzing the financial affairs of the victim to assist a police investigation, the forensic accountant may seek to determine the following:

1. The victim's business relationships and the identity of people with whom he had dealings
2. Whether any debts were owed by the victim and whether evidence exists to suggest the victim was either resisting or had an inability to pay them
3. Whether any debts were owed to the victim and whether evidence exists to suggest that the debtor was resisting payment on them
4. Whether a financial motive can be eliminated as a direction to pursue in the investigation
5. Whether other motives may exist

6.9.1.1 *Regina v. Serplus.* In Regina v. William Serplus, it was alleged that Serplus murdered Muriel MacIntosh, an aging prostitute with whom he had lived for two years, for the purpose of appropriating certain of her assets to his own use. Those assets included a collection of Royal Doulton figurines valued at over $100,000, MacIntosh's private home in Toronto with an equity of $35,000, and certain jewelry items.

Serplus had met MacIntosh at the Warwick Hotel in Toronto during the fall of 1979. MacIntosh used the hotel as her point of solicitations. She and Serplus became friendly and MacIntosh confided that because of her age (54), she felt she couldn't go on much longer as a prostitute. She wanted to get involved in some other line of work. Serplus installed a security system in MacIntosh's home at 151 Gilmour, and shortly thereafter he moved in with her.

Throughout the next two years, Serplus derived a number of financial benefits from his relationship with MacIntosh. He apparently convinced her she should invest her money in his new venture, the Triple S Holding Company. From time to time during their cohabitation, MacIntosh also advanced money to Serplus either for "investment" or other purposes. A schedule of such benefits and the documentation used as proof at the trial of William Serplus are shown in Exhibits 6.8, 6.9, 6.10 and 6.11.

Sometime during the evening of November 18, 1980, or the early morning of November 19, 1980, Muriel MacIntosh was beaten, tied, and strangled with an electrical cord. About two months later her body was found in a garage at the rear of her home, frozen solid in a blue steamer trunk. (Friends had notified police she was missing.) She was dressed in a nightgown with a wool sweater over it, and around her upper body was a green Glad bag that matched a package of trash bags found in the kitchen of her residence. Paint on the electrical cord matched the paint in the back bedroom of the house, and the string used was matched to a ball of string located in one of the kitchen cupboards.

On November 20, 1980, Serplus rented a van and a hand dolly from Sommerville Rental at Bloor and High Park in Toronto. Around noon two witnesses saw Serplus coming from 151 Gilmour Avenue with a blue steamer trunk on a hand dolly. The van was parked opposite the house. It appeared to the witnesses that Serplus was unable to load the truck into the rear of the van. He was seen wheeling the trunk north on Gilmour Avenue and around the corner toward the alleyway leading to the garage at the rear of 151 Gilmour. The Canadian Centre for Forensic Sciences found blood and paint from the

Date	Schedule Number		Amount
1979			
December 27	I	CIBC cable of funds	$ 5,000.00
1980			
January 7	I	CIBC cable of funds	1,491.00
March 25	I	Cash value from insurance	1,700.00
September 17	I	CNCP money transfer	350.00
September 25	I	CNCP money transfer	165.00
June 27	II	Cash deposit to Triple S Holding	6,000.00
November 11	II	Equity transferred on 151 Gilmour Avenue	35,000.00
November 18	III	Cash from Royal Doulton figurines	550.00
November 20	III	Cash from Royal Doulton figurines	2,500.00
November 21	III	Cash from Royal Doulton figurines	9,225.00
			$61,981.00

EXHIBIT 6.8. A summary of transactions set out on schedules I, II, and III which appear to indicate benefit to or on behalf of William Serplus.

steamer trunk on the hand dolly. On that same day, Serplus received $2,500 in cash from Charlton's as a partial payment on the Royal Doulton collection of figurines.

On Friday, November 21, 1980, Serplus went to Ivan's Jewelry Store on Bloor Street West and spoke with Teresa Bellovits, the owner of the store. There he ordered a wedding ring he said was for a niece who was getting married in the States. He also purchased a Bulova wristwatch for himself. He showed Bellovits seven rings he had in his possession plus a very expensive watch he was trying to sell. Bellovits purchased two of the rings and a set of earrings from Serplus for $3,500.

On November 22, 1980, Serplus met with a Mr. Cross from Charltons and was paid $9,225 as the final installment for the Royal Doulton collection. Serplus later went to his office and showed his secretary the money. That evening Serplus met Bellovits for supper and then went back to her house and spent the night.

A week later on November 29, 1980, Serplus married a local school teacher in Scranton, Pennsylvania. They honeymooned in Puerto Rico, and on their return to Scranton lived together in her apartment until his arrest. Meanwhile in Toronto several of Muriel MacIntosh's friends contacted the police to file missing person report. On December 30, 1980, the police received a call from

Date			
1979			
December	27	A Canadian Imperial Bank of Commerce payment by cable #CT0270007 in the amount of Canadian $5,000.00 from Miss Muriel MacIntosh is paid to the benefit of William Serplus via Canadian Imperial Bank of Commerce, Nassau, Bahamas.	$5,000.00
1980			
January	7	A Canadian Imperial Bank of Commerce payment by cable #CT0270008 in the amount of Canadian $1,491.00 from Miss Muriel MacIntosh is paid to the benefit of William Serplus via Canadian Imperial Bank of Commerce, Nassau, Bahamas.	1,491.00
March	25	An Independent Order of Foresters check #1-0152186 in the amount of $1,700.00 is payable to the order of John McCrady. The back of the check bears an endorsement by a John McCrady and a bank stamp which is dated March 26, 1980, indicating a deposit to the Royal Bank account #5921028 in the name of William Serplus. The Royal Bank statement for account #5921028 in the name of William Serplus indicates a deposit of $1,700.00.	1,700.00
September	17	A CNCP money transfer #X4950475 in the amount of Canadian $350.00 is made by Muriel MacIntosh payable to William Serplus, Scranton, PA.	350.00
September	25	A CNCP money transfer #X4951019 in the amount of Canadian $165.00 is made by Muriel McIntosh payable to William Serplus, Scranton, PA.	165.00

EXHIBIT 6.9. A listing of documentation that benefits William Serplus.

a male who identified himself as William Serplus calling from New York City. He informed the officer that MacIntosh had gone to the East Coast to visit her brother. He also stated he would be in Toronto January 6 and would come to see the officer on January 7. He failed to show up. The police arrested him a few days later.

6.9.2 Arson for Profit

Arson for profit and planned bankruptcy share some similar characteristics. In both situations business problems exist and are acknowledged to exist by

Date			
1980			

June 19   A "Real Estate Appraiser's Report" indicates an appraised value for the land and building at 151 Gilmour Avenue of an amount of $70,000.00.

June 27   A mortgage in the amount of $35,000.00 is obtained by Muriel MacIntosh from the Premier Trust Company secured by the Gilmour Avenue property.

June 27   A "Statement of Trust Distribution" prepared by Nakelsky, Barrister and Solicitor, which sets out the disbursement of the $35,000.00 mortgage proceeds notes "paid to Muriel Grace MacIntosh $9,839.13."

June 27   A trust check #4078 in the amount of $9,839.13 drawn on the account of David Nakelsky, Barrister and Solicitor, is issued to the order of Muriel MacIntosh. The back of the check bears the endorsement Muriel MacIntosh. The deposit of this check could not be identified in any of the known bank accounts of Muriel MacIntosh.

June 27   A Guaranty Trust deposit slip for account #900357 in the name of Triple S Holding Company indicates a deposit of $6,000.00 cash composed of six $1,000.00 bills. A review of the accounts payable listing and the bank statement in the name of Triple S Holding Company appears to suggest that the funds were applied to cover the following disbursements: **$ 6,000.00**

Sources:

June 24	Beginning bank balance	$ 153.05
June 27	Deposit	6,000.00
		$6,153.05

Applications:

June 30	Cash (June 30)	$2,000.00
June 30	The Bay (June 28)	300.00
July 3	Cash (July 3)	500.00
July 3	Public Optical (June 27)	40.50
July 3	Noia Tax & Accounting Services re rent (July 1)	185.00

July	3	Public Optical (June 27)	76.50
July	10	Cash (July 4)	500.00
July	10	Toronto Hydro (June 25)	25.19
July	15	Cash (July 14)	1,500.00
July	15	Ind. Order of Foresters (July)	119.52
July	15	S/C	1.28
July	15	Ending bank balance	905.06
			$6,153.05

November 11	A deed of land indicates a conveyance by Muriel MacIntosh of the property identified as 151 Gilmour Avenue to Triple S Holding Company Limited in consideration for "monies paid or to be paid in cash $35,000.00" with a further notation "gift from shareholder to corporation." It would appear that the amount of $35,000.00 represents the difference between the appraisal value of the property and the amount of the existing mortgage with Premier Trust Company.	$35,000.00
November 12	Triple S Holding Company Limited is incorporated with William Serplus noted as the first director and shareholder of the company, holding 304,000 shares.	

1980

November 17	A Charlton International Publishing Inc. purchase order #NP1390 indicates a purchase from William Serplus of Royal Doulton figurines for an amount of $11,725.00. Notations on this document indicate payment in cash as follows:	

November 20, 1980	$ 2,500.00	$ 2,500.00
November 22, 1980	9,225.00	9,225.00
	$11,725.00	

November 18	A Charlton International Publishing Inc. purchase order #NP7108 indicates the purchase of "6 figurines" for an amount of $550.00.	550.00
November 25	A loan ledger of the First National Bank, Dunmore, PA indicates a loan in the amount of $3,000.00 granted to William Serplus and bears the notation: "$9000 Canadian money collateral."	

EXHIBIT 6.10. A listing of documentation in regard to 151 Gilmour Avenue, Toronto, Ontario.

Date 1980		
May	14	A Tippet—Richardson Limited storage order form in the name of Mr. M. Constantineau c/o Miss Muriel MacIntosh indicates the storage of 200 pieces of Royal Doulton and an insurance value of $100,000.00.
June	2	A Tippet—Richardson Limited invoice #3962 to Mr. M. Constantineau makes reference to nine large china packs.
September	30	A Tippet—Richardson Limited document indicates delivery of the nine cartons to Miss Muriel MacIntosh at 151 Gilmour Avenue in Toronto with the move to occur on October 2, 1980.
November	11	A document signed Miss Muriel Grace MacIntosh under the date of November 12, 1980, states in part, "I, Muriel Grace MacIntosh, hereby do assign to be used for capitalization, Triple S Holding Co. Ltd. for one share, at no par value, Two Hundred and Twenty-five Thousand Dollars of Royal Doulton figurines . . ." Listed thereafter are the names of the Royal Doulton figurines collection.

EXHIBIT 6.11. A listing of documentation regarding the Royal Doulton collection

management. Arson, like planned bankruptcy, can become the means for making the best of a bad situation.

The role of the forensic accountant in arson-related matters is to determine the present business position of the company and its owners. Although the financial position may have a considerable bearing on motive, motive is better understood in the context of the business itself and the owners through a review of all aspects of the operations and ownership of the business. Accordingly it is usually appropriate to obtain as much background information as possible. A starting point might be the date of acquisition of an established business or the commencement date of a new business venture. A review of the annual financial statements and associated working papers since acquisition may disclose the company's yearly performance and any underlying business problems.

Any review of the status of a business must be objective. It should identify not only matters unfavorable to management and the owners of the company but also matters that are favorable. The unfavorable matters may well be obvious (e.g., steady decline in sales, worsening creditor relations, or a significant withdrawal of funds immediately before the fire). On the other hand, the owner may have put a substantial amount of his or her own money into the business shortly before the fire.

A review of the recent court cases show that the main characteristics to be considered and established as evidence of arson are as follows:

1. Ownership
2. Financial motive
3. Existence of an insurance policy
4. The establishment of exclusive opportunity
5. The origin of the fire as incendiary

Accountants can assist with investigation of the first three of these issues and in particular ownership and financial motive. They can analyze information from several sources to construct a chronology of the financial records of the owner, the business, and third parties; and demonstrate the company's position at the time of the fire in comparison with earlier periods. The initial sources of documents are those financial and accounting records of the business that were not destroyed. Beyond this the accountant should seek information from others directly or indirectly connected with the business. Such sources may include the company's banker, lawyer, accountant, customers, suppliers, insurers, and government agencies and realtors. The business owner should always be given the opportunity to volunteer any personal or business records he might have.

A list of key questions to be considered by the forensic accountant and documents to be examined follows:

1. Who maintained the accounting records?
2. What accounting records were kept that would have been available if not destroyed in the fire?
3. What is the ownership structure and form of organization?
4. Is the financial position of the owner solid? How about the entity itself?
5. Does the business support the owner?
6. Does the owner support the business?

7. Has the owner had any past connection with failed business ventures?

8. What is the history and pattern of earnings?

9. Could ownership benefit from "selling out" to the insurance company?

10. Did any significant events relating to the owner or the business occur at or around the time of the fire?

11. Who are the major suppliers and what were the business's relations with them?

12. Who are the major customers and what were the business's relations with them?

13. Who are the bankers and what were the business's relations with them?

14. Who is the external accountant?

15. Who is the corporate solicitor?

16. Has the business recently been offered for sale or had negotiations to sell failed?

17. Have there been any recent changes in insurance coverage?

Third party documents that should be sought include:

1. Filings for incorporation, partnership, or assumed names

2. Deeds, mortgages, and liens on real estate

3. Chattel mortgage filings

4. Accountant's working paper files

5. Tax returns

6. Correspondence with customers and suppliers

7. Bank credit files

8. Credit files from other creditors

9. Bank statements, deposit slips, credit/debit memos (paper or micro-fiche records)

10. Bank statements and canceled checks not mailed out

11. Payroll information from employees

12. Attorney's closing files and trust ledger sheets (escrow accounts)

13. Real estate listings

6.9.3 Commercial Bribery (Secret Commissions)

Simply defined, secret commissions (or bribery) represent payments or the provision of goods, services, advantage, or benefit of any kind in return for actual or perceived advantage, benefit, or preferential treatment. The relevant section of the Criminal Code of Canada (383) does not require that a secret commission be given; it need only be offered or demanded. In any event essentially two parties are involved: the payor and the recipient. The payor, through actual or potential relationships with the principal (e.g., employer) of the recipient, has or wishes to obtain a benefit, advantage, or preferential treatment. For example, Company A (the payor) wishes to sell its product to Company B (the principal). The recipient is a person in a position of authority or influence in the affairs of his principal (employer), or is perceived to be in such a position. The payor wishes to obtain the benefit of preferential treatment through the recipient. The recipient may be a senior officer, a purchasing manager, or someone with control over company assets, including their acquisition or disposal.

Many companies today issue codes of ethics that must be adhered to by employees. Acknowledgement is usually required, evidenced by the employee's signature. These codes often prohibit the acceptance of gifts and gratuities, or permit employees to accept only those below a certain value. Employees may also be prohibited from taking actions that constitute a conflict with the employer's interests.

The payor may rationalize the offer or payment of a secret commission as necessary to obtain new business or to maintain the status quo in existing business relationships. Thus the payor may view the transaction as being in the normal course of business. The recipient will rationalize receipt of the payment especially if he or she had recently been denied a promotion or pay raise. The secret commission may be part of a larger criminal act. A secret commission may be offered or paid to gain the cooperation or acquiescence of the recipient so that a fraud can be perpetrated on the recipient's principal.

The secret commission may be a straightforward cash transaction directly between the payor and the recipient. Or goods and services might be provided, such as travel or gifts, at no cost or reduced cost. The commission could also be paid indirectly through related companies or businesses of the payor and/or recipient, often in foreign jurisdictions. The indirect route is taken to lend the appearance of legitimacy or to disguise the transaction.

The investigative accountant must resolve several issues. He or she must:

1. Determine the nature of the relationship between the payor and the recipient and his principal. This is crucial to establishing the motive for the payment of the alleged secret commission.

2. Determine the recipient's relationship with his principal and with the alleged payor in order to establish whether and how the recipient could influence the affairs of his principal.

3. Identify all related companies or businesses of the payor and the recipient. The payor may not necessarily be the person or company receiving the advantage, benefit, or preferential treatment granted by the recipient, it may be a subsidiary company. Also, the recipient may not receive the secret commission directly.

4. Determine the form and the purpose of the alleged secret commission. This usually involves a review of the accounting and banking records of both the payor and the recipient.

The accounting records will be extremely important in the investigation of the issues discussed earlier. The investigative accountant can assist in several ways, including the following:

1. Examine the financial records of the payor and the principal to establish the nature of the relationships (e.g., supplier/customer) and the extent of their dealings. The records may disclose the bid process or other purchasing process.

2. Investigate the personal financial affairs of the recipient to help establish a motive. Analysis of the records may help establish a life-style inconsistent with income and hence a need for personal gain.

3. Establish whether the recipient has any power to authorize transactions and what the power is. He or she may be authorized to sign checks, authorize purchases, or grant credit, for example, up to a certain limit. Has the limit been strictly observed?

4. Uncover loans or advances related to the principal or to the payor by examining audit work and tax returns.

5. Establish whether the alleged secret commission takes the form of cash or payments to the benefit of the recipient (e.g., travel, car, etc.). The books of account of the payor or of the appropriate related company will

have to be reviewed for supporting documentation, such as checks or supplier invoices. The review should also disclose how such payments were recorded by the payor.

For example, if the payment is recorded as an expense, the auditor will:

1. Establish the nature of the expense (e.g., promotion, travel, etc.) and whether such payments reflect the normal course of business or indicate an unusual transaction.
2. Obtain documents such as an invoice, purchase order, contract, or shipping document that describes the goods or services being paid for.

If the payment is recorded as a loan to the recipient, the investigator should consider the following:

1. What was the purpose of the loan?
2. Does a promissory note exist?
3. Has any interest been charged on the loan, and has any interest been collected?
4. What are the terms of repayment, if any, and have any payments been made?
5. If the loan has been repaid, was a check presented for payment, and did it properly clear the banking system?

If the alleged secret commission is in the form of cash, the recipient's bank records should be reviewed to identify, if possible, unaccountable deposits to his or her account. It would also be useful to review the recipient's known assets. How and when were such assets acquired and what documentation is available in support? It is possible that payment has been made to a bank account in a foreign jurisdiction to the benefit of the recipient.

The alleged secret commission may appear to be a normal business transaction for normal business purposes. However, the substance of the transaction must be determined. In addition, does the alleged secret commission coincide with an event or transaction that, because of the relationship between the payor and the recipient and his principal, results in an actual or potential benefit?

6.9.3.1 *Red Flags of Commercial Billing.* The accountant should be aware c those situations that might disclose possible kickbacks. Here are some example:

1. Unaccounted-for cash; assets such as house, cottage, or car; or lifestyle—expensive vacations, gambling—of the recipient

2. Unusual transactions or unusual changes in the activity of the *princip* of the recipient: Unusual transactions are those that deviate from nor mal business practice or price; changes might include a switch of majc suppliers unaccounted for by price or quality

3. Payments to a business or company owned or controlled by the recip ent or to a non-arm's-length partner, such as a spouse

4. Acts by an employee beyond the scope of his normal responsibilities approve or influence the approval of transactions

6.9.3.2 *Regina v. Campbell and Mitchell.* At a social function in 1983 director of a major retailer was told that there were possible irregularities the retailer's purchasing function. The director was told that certain tc suppliers were having considerable difficulty in presenting their products fc consideration by the retailer.

As a result of preliminary investigations by the retailer, it was suspecte that Campbell, its director of buying for toys and related products, possib had ownership interests in companies that sold products to the retailer. The companies were apparently operated by Mitchell, a supplier of toys and agent for numerous toy manufacturers.

Police searches were executed on Campbell's office at the company, t business premises of Mitchell's companies, Campbell's personal residenc Mitchell's personal residence, and the offices of the various accountants a lawyers related by Mitchell's companies.

Campbell had signed annual conflict-of-interest statements that did n disclose transactions with or ownership interest in companies dealing with t retailers. Twelve companies were owned to some extent by some combinati of Campbell and his wife and Mitchell and his wife. These companies report approximately $6 million in sales for the period 1976 to 1983. More than percent of this amount was attributable to transactions with the retaile Campbell and his wife received over $500,000 and Mitchell and his wife ov $700,000 in cash and benefits from Mitchell companies.

The report of the forensic accountant, supported by multivolume briefs of ocuments, included:

1. Corporate structure charts that outlined the ownership history and relationships between the Mitchell companies
2. Summarized chronologies by each individual Mitchell company outlining corporate ownership, transactions with the retailer, and benefits received by Campbell and Mitchell and their wives

The defense counsel concentrated on the following activities:

1. Confirming that the books and records of the Mitchell companies were reasonably maintained and complete
2. Confirming that the wives of Campbell and Mitchell were inactive in the operations of the Mitchell companies
3. Confirming that the income and benefits received from the Mitchell companies by the individuals were properly and fully disclosed in the individuals' personal tax returns
4. Establishing that the number of companies and the changing interrelationships were primarily for tax planning purposes
5. Establishing that there was no evidence Mitchell knew that Campbell had not disclosed to the retailer Campbell's ownership interest and benefits related to the Mitchell companies
6. Establishing that there was no evidence of any financial loss to the retailer related to its transactions with the Mitchell companies
7. Establishing that Campbell was not active in the Mitchell companies
8. Establishing that the buyers reporting to Campbell, not Campbell himself, were responsible for the retailer purchases from the Mitchell companies
9. Establishing that the financial records indicated that Campbell had little responsibility for purchases by the retailer made from the Mitchell companies on reorders rather than initial orders

The trial judge concluded that Campbell and Mitchell were guilty as harged. The judge outlined the rationale for the law related to secret commissions. In brief it is to protect the principal (in this case, the retailer) from secret and dishonest acts of its agents (in this case, Campbell). The judge concluded that a principal-and-agent relationship clearly existed in this case. The judge then concentrated on the following matters:

1. The offense requires that benefits/considerations pass from the offerer to the acceptor in a corrupt or *mala fide* manner. (In this matter the Court must conclude whether corrupt intent existed, if only "reasonable inference" is submitted as evidence.)

2. There was no direct evidence that the benefits were passed corruptly. All consideration and benefits were recorded in the books and records of the Mitchell companies and in the personal tax returns of the Campbells and Mitchell.

3. Further, there was no direct evidence that Campbell routed the retailer's business to the Mitchell companies. Also, there was no direct evidence that Mitchell knew of Campbell's nondisclosure to the retailer of his conflicts of interest.

But the trial judge concluded that Campbell's opportunity and motive did support the reasonable inference that Campbell routed the retailer's business to the Mitchell-related companies. The trial judge further concluded that Campbell's and Mitchell's long-standing social and business relationship, and the nature and extent of business done by the Campbell—Mitchell companies with the retailer, allowed the reasonable inference that Mitchell understood Campbell's role and responsibilities as the retailer. Together with Campbell's nondisclosure to the retailer of his conflict of interest, these reasonable inferences led the trial judge to conclude that benefits were passed to Campbell in a corrupt or *mala fide* manner.

7

THE ACCOUNTANT/AUDITOR AS AN EXPERT WITNESS

Lay witnesses are generally restricted from testifying in the form of opinions, conclusions, and characterizations. Laypersons may, however, express opinions in the limited sense of estimating the speed of a moving vehicle, approximating temperature and distances, identifying common smells, and testifying in matters of physical description such as age, height, and weight.

But qualified experts may give their professional opinions. Consider the following Michigan Supreme Court Rules of Evidence on this point:[1]

Rule 702   Testimony by Experts

If the court determines that recognized scientific, technical, or other specialized knowledge will assist the trier of fact to understand the evidence or to determine a fact in issue, a witness qualified as an expert by knowledge, skill, experience, training, or education, may testify thereto in the form of an opinion or otherwise.

Rule 703   Bases of Opinion Testimony by Experts

The facts or data in the particular case upon which an expert bases an opinion or inference may be those perceived by or made known to him at or before the hearing. The court may require that underlying facts or data essential to an opinion or inference be in evidence.

Rule 704   Opinion on Ultimate Issue

Testimony in the form of an opinion or inference otherwise admissible is not objectionable because it embraces an ultimate issue to be decided by the trier of fact.

Rule 705   *Disclosure of Facts or Data Underlying Expert Opinion*

The expert may testify in terms of opinion or inference and give his reasons therefor without prior disclosure of the underlying facts or data, unless the court requires otherwise. The expert may in any event be required to disclose the underlying facts or data on cross-examination.

Rule 706   *Court-Appointed Experts*

(a) *Appointment*. The court may on its own motion or on the motion of any party enter an order to show cause why expert witnesses should be appointed, and may request the parties to submit nominations. The court may appoint any expert witnesses agreed upon by the parties, and may appoint expert witnesses of its own selection. An expert witness shall not be appointed by the court unless he consents to act. A witness so appointed shall be informed of his duties by the court in writing, a copy of which shall be filed with the clerk, or at a conference in which the parties shall have opportunity to participate. A witness so appointed shall advise the parties of his findings, if any, his deposition may be taken by any party, and he may be called to testify by the court or any party. He shall be subject to cross-examination by each party, including a party calling him as a witness.

(b) *Compensation*. Expert witnesses so appointed are entitled to reasonable compensation in whatever sum the court may allow. The compensation thus fixed is payable from funds which may be provided by law in criminal cases and civil actions and proceedings involving just compensation under the Fifth Amendment. In other civil actions and proceedings the compensation shall be paid by the parties in such proportion and at such time as the court directs, and thereafter charged in like manner as other costs.

(c) *Disclosure of appointment*. In the exercise of its discretion, the court may authorize disclosure to the jury of the fact that the court appointed the expert witness.

(d) *Parties experts of own selection*. Nothing in this rule limits the parties in calling expert witnesses of their own selection.

Rule 707   *Use of Learned Treatises for Impeachment*

To the extent called to the attention of an expert witness upon cross-examination or relied upon by him in direct examination, statements contained in published treatises, periodicals, or pamphlets on a subject of history, medicine, or other science or art, established as a reliable authority by the testimony or admission of the witness or by other expert testimony or by judicial notice, are admissible for impeachment purposes only.

Expert witnesses may be cross-examined as any other witness and especially as to qualifications, bases of opinions, and compensation for testifying.

Expert witnesses may express opinions in response to hypothetical questions, if the hypothesized facts in the questions are supported by the evidence of the case.

Accountants and auditors are often called upon to provide testimony in litigation support matters and criminal prosecutions in which their services are utilized to support investigations of such crimes as financial frauds, embezzlement, misapplication of funds, arson for profit, bankruptcy fraud, and tax evasion. Accountants and auditors may also be utilized as defense witnesses or as support to the defendant's counsel on matters that involve accounting or audit issues.

7.1 QUALIFICATION AND ADMISSIBILITY OF ACCOUNTING SCHEDULES

qualify accountants and auditors as technical experts is generally not a ficult task. Questions are posed to them concerning their professional edentials (i.e., education, work experience, licensing or certification, hnical-training courses taken, technical books and journal articles written, ices held in professional associations, and awards and commendations ceived).

Defense lawyers are generally not prone to challenge the expertise of countants and auditors, assuming they meet at least minimum standards of ofessional competence. To do so may give these experts an opportunity to ly highlight their professional credentials and perhaps make a greater pression on the jury or judge, thus adding more weight to their testimony. defense attorneys often pass on the opportunity to challenge these expert tnesses.

What accountants and auditors testify to in general are their investigative dings, if called by the prosecution, and, if called by the defense, they may tify about the quality of the findings or the opinions expressed by the osecution's accounting expert, in order to create doubt in the minds of mbers of the jury about the credibility or weight to give to the prosecu- n's expert.

To become a credible expert accounting witness, one must be generally knowledgeable in his or her own field by education and experience, be member in good standing of the profession, or some specialized aspect practice within the profession if pertinent to the case at hand. But there a other considerations as well to make an expert witness credible. The expe will appear credible when he or she follows these suggestions:

1. Speak clearly and audibly.
2. Refrain from using professional jargon.
3. Use simple rather than complex terms to describe findings a opinions.
4. Speak to the specific questions asked; do not go off on tangents volunteer more than a question asks.
5. Do not verbally fence with the defense attorney or prosecutor.
6. Look directly at the question poser (prosecutor or defense counse
7. Maintain a professional demeanor, do not smile gratuitously at t judge, jury, the lawyer who hired you, or the opponent's counse
8. Be calm and deliberate in responding to questions, speak neither t slowly nor too rapidly.
9. Dress conservatively.
10. Have hair neatly combed and shoes newly shined.
11. Use graphs, charts, and other visual aids if they help to clarify a poi
12. Do not read from notes if you can avoid it. (The opposition lawyer v probably demand to see such notes if you do, and you will then look if you rehearsed your testimony).
13. If you have documents to introduce, have them organized so that y can quickly retrieve them when asked to do so by the counsel whose side you are testifying.
14. Do not "hem and haw" or stammer. Retain your composure whe tough or complex question is posed.
15. Ask for repetition or clarification if you do not fully understand question.
16. If you do not know the answer, say so—don't guess.
17. In cross-examination do not respond too quickly. Counsel for your s may wish to interpose an objection to the question.

18. If the judge elects to ask a question, respond to it by looking at him or her.

19. Do not stare off into space, or at the floor or ceiling.

20. Be friendly to all sides.

21. Do not raise your voice in anger if the opponent's lawyer tries to bait you.

22. Be honest. Don't invent. Don't inflate. Don't evade.

The goal of the forensic accountant is to make his or her findings under-
andable to counsel, judges, and juries, and to avoid resorting to jargon and
ademic polemics about accounting rules and standards. The facts, stated
mply and briefly, are all the audience needs or cares to hear. Anything
yond that only makes accounting and auditing more obscure.

7.1.1 Qualifying as an Expert Witness

he extract reproduced from the proceedings in *Regina* v. *Scheel* shows how
e accountant's qualifications as an expert witness can be established and how
counting exhibits might be introduced.

Robert John Lindquist: Sworn
Examination-in-Chief by Mr. Hunt (Crown):

Q. Mr. Lindquist, where do you reside, sir?

A. I live in Toronto, Ontario.

Q. And what is your occupation?

A. I am a chartered accountant.

Q. And do you practice on your own or with someone else?

A. I practice in partnership with other chartered accountants under the firm name of Lindquist, Holmes, and Company.

Q. And how long have you been operating the partnership as a chartered accountant?

A. Close to six years now.

Q. And prior to that were you associated with any other firm?

A. Yes, prior to that I worked for a period of six years with a national accounting firm where I studied after my graduation from University.

Q. And in what year did you qualify as a chartered accountant?

A. In 1972.

Q. And since that date have you had occasion to testify in court with respect to accounting matters?

A. I have.

Q. And on approximately how many occasions would that have occurred?

A. An estimate of some 50 occasions.

Mr. Hunt: Your Honor, I tender Mr. Lindquist as a witness who should be classified as an expert witness on the basis of his qualifications that I have elicited.

Mr. Hermiston: I am content with the qualifications, Your Honor.

His Honor: Thank you.

Mr. Hunt: Mr. Lindquist, I understand that you have prepared a number of documents relating to various transactions dealing with Metro Pallet Repair?

A. Yes, I have.

Q. Could I see Exhibit A? I am presenting to you a document, a rather large document, marked Exhibit A on the Voir Dire. I would ask you to look at that document and tell me if you recognize that?

A. Yes, I do.

Q. And did you prepare that document yourself?

A. Yes, I did.

Q. And I wonder if, so the jury can see it, you would hold it in such a way that the jury will be able to see the structure of the document. It appears to consist of a number of columns, vertical columns; am I correct?

A. That's correct.

Q. And the document is headed what?

A. It's headed, "Analysis of Sales for the Period August 1, 1973, to October 3 1973."[2]

7.1.2 Admissibility of Accounting Evidence

Documentary accounting evidence may be presented in a court of law in forms: (1) primary, such as original, individual accounting documents tained from the parties concerned or other sources, and (2) secondary summaries and schedules based on the original documents. These are duced by an accountant based upon an examination of the primary evider

The issue of whether secondary accounting evidence should be admissible as been argued in courts of law for many years. Rulings in several Canadian ses have helped clarify the admissibility of this type of evidence.

In *Regina v. Harold Scheel*, for example the ruling allowed that a summary documentary evidence was admissible. However, it was ruled that a mmary was in itself not evidence, but an aid to understanding primary idence that had already been adduced. The judge determined regarding e use of secondary evidence that no more reliance could be placed on this idence than was placed on the primary evidence.

The following has been extracted from the Ontario Court of Appeal's cision in *Regina v. Scheel*:

The only ground of appeal advanced by counsel on the appellant's appeal from conviction upon which we think it is necessary to comment, relates to the admission of evidence of certain summaries, which it was contended, were not admissible. The summaries in question were prepared by Mr. R. Lindquist, a Chartered Accountant, who testified that he prepared them from the following sources: (a) exhibits, (b) the agreed statement of facts, (c) the testimony at the trial, and (d) evidence given at the preliminary hearing read in at the trial.

The first and most important summary to which objection was taken is a document with respect to Metro Pallet Repair Company entitled "Analysis of Sales for the Period August 1, 1973, to October 5, 1973." This summary lists by customer the number of boxes (pallets) ordered by the customer as per a numbered invoice. The analysis gives the history of the order, showing the number of boxes covered by the invoice, the amount of money paid by the customer, the number of boxes delivered, the value of the boxes delivered, the number of boxes not delivered, and the amount of money not returned (i.e. the money received less the amount represented by the value of the boxes delivered). The analysis also shows the accumulated total of unfilled orders in relation to all customers who placed orders for boxes during the period, as well as the accumulated total of unreturned payments in relation to all customers during the period.

The second summary of schedule is a "Statement of Known Receipts and Disbursements for the Period August 1, 1973, to October 5, 1973." This document shows the total receipts and disbursements for the period, the funds processed through the bank, the funds not processed through the bank, and the amount of money unaccounted for.

The third summary is entitled "Accounts Receivable in Process as of August 27, 1973." This summary lists by customer the number of boxes (pallets) ordered, their value, the percentage complete and delivered, and the deposits received on account as of August 27, 1973. Mr. Leslie contended that the summaries were not admissible, that the original documents from which they were compiled constituted the best evidence, and that the summary would tend to overwhelm the jury.

We are all of the view that the summaries, based on evidence which had been properly admitted, were admissible to assist the jury in understanding the entire picture represented by voluminous documentary evidence. The useful-ness of the summaries depends entirely, however, upon the acceptance by the jury of the proof of the facts upon which the summaries were based.

The admissibility of evidence of this type does not appear to have been pre-viously considered by any appellate court in Canada in a reported judgment. In *R. v. Parks* (unreported, released March 18, 1974) His Honor Judge Moore, presiding in the Court of General Sessions of the Peace for the County of Grey, held that a summary of documentary evidence based upon a "veritable blizzard of documents" prepared by Mr. Lindquist was admissible. The decision of His Honor Judge Moore was followed by His Honor Judge Graburn, presiding in the Court of General Sessions of the Peace for the Judicial District of York, in *R. v. Steel and Waddilove* (unreported May 5, 1976).

The admissibility of such evidence is well established in the United States. In *Hoyer v. United States*, 8 Cir., 223 F. 2d 134 (1955) the Court held that in a prosecution for attempting to evade income taxes, summaries prepared from documentary and oral evidence were admissible to show the defendant's correct net income. Gardner, Chief Judge, delivering the judgment of the Court said:[3] ". . . these exhibits so compiled and prepared purported to show the correct net income of the defendant for the years covered by the indictment. They were prepared by experts from documentary evidence introduced and from oral testimony. As the documentary evidence had already been introduced counsel for the defendant had ample opportunity to examine it and to cross-examine the expert as to the basic testimony and his calculations based thereon. The evi-dence was clearly admissible.

The documentary evidence presented a complicated situation and required elaborate compilations which could not have been made by the jury. It is also to be noted in this connection that the Court advised the jury that the testimony of the experts was advisory and need not be accepted by them as a variety."

In *Daniel v. United States* 5 Cir., 343 F. 2d 785 (1965) Hunter, District Judge delivering the judgment of the Court, said:[4]

. . . "The rule is that a summary of books and records is admissible, provided cross-examination is allowed and the original records are available. Here the records of which the exhibits are summaries were in evidence, and the man who prepared them was available for cross-examination.

It is perfectly proper that litigants be permitted the use of illustrative charts to summarize varying computations and to thus make the primary proof upon which such charts must be based more enlightening to the jury. The district judge did not abuse his discretion by permitting the use of these summaries.

I would also observe that in the present case the summaries were helpful to the appellant, with respect to some of the counts.

The introduction of the summaries did not offend against the rule that requires the production of original documents, since the documents which were the primary source of the summaries were in evidence. It is accordingly unnecessary in this case to invoke the exception to the rule referred to by Wigmore in the following passage:

Where a fact could be ascertained only by the inspection of a large number of documents made up of very *numerous detailed shipments* . . . as the net balance resulting from a year's vouchers of a treasurer or a year's accounts in a bank ledger—it is obvious that it would often be practically out of the question to apply the present principle by requiring the production of the entire mass of documents and entries to be perused by the jury or read aloud to them. The convenience of trials demands that other evidence be allowed to be offered, in the shape of the testimony of a competent witness who has perused the entire mass and will state summarily the net result. Such a practice is well established to be proper.

Most courts require, as a condition, that the mass thus summarily testified to shall, if the occasion seems to require it, be placed at hand in court, or at least be made accessible to the opposing party, in order that the correctness of the evidence may be tested by inspection if desired, or that the material for cross-examination may be made available. . . ."

Accordingly, we were of the view that the learned trial judge did not err in admitting the summaries previously described.

7.2 PROFILE OF THE EXPERT WITNESS

An expert witness in the area of accounting must have a thorough knowledge not only generally accepted accounting principles but also the current promulgations of his or her institute. Often the expert's expertise may involve special knowledge of a specific industry, such as construction accounting or accounting in a stock market environment. In this case, the expert should be aware of recent developments and any important accounting issues within that area.

The expert must also be analytical and possess the ability to work with incomplete data. The expert may, however, not always be able to recognize

when data is incomplete. As a result, the expert may make various assum
tions that would then be open for interpretation or attack. If all data has *n*
been made available, then it is quite possible that the opposing counsel m:
be able to offer alternate scenarios that are more plausible under the circu
stances, thus discrediting the expert.

The expert must have the ability to simplify complex issues. It is helpful
the expert can communicate in a very direct and simple manner, keeping
mind that he or she is communicating with nonaccountants and that t
expert's role as noted above is to clarify complex issues to allow everyone
understand them. In view of this, some background or experience in teachi
is often of assistance.

The question often arises as to whether or not being a Chartered Accou
tant is sufficient to qualify oneself as an expert. Generally, a person *may* be
expert in his particular field of expertise if he has sufficient experience and
member of his or her institute. This does not mean that a Chartered Accou
tant is automatically an expert; however, it passes the first hurdle. It is m
helpful to have prior experience with litigation or criminal matters to
considered an expert. This is primarily as a result of the awareness tha
instilled during the testifying experience. Further, it is often of assistance
have been accepted as an expert in other matters, thereby easing curr
acceptance. A danger exists, however, of appearing to be an expert at being
expert witness.

Often, the counsel introducing the witness will read the expert's qualif
tions or ask specific questions of the witness to establish his or her credenti
On occasion, the qualifications of the expert witness are read directly into
court record. Although the expert's qualifications are not often contested,
a distinct possibility. Over and above being accepted by both parties,
expert witness most importantly must be accepted by the court.

7.3 ROLE PLAYED IN LITIGATION TEAM

Generally, the expert plays an ongoing part of the litigation team. In part
lar, the expert's involvement may be at various stages throughout the de
opment of the case, most notably:

1. Case assessment
2. Identification of documentation required to support the case, I
   additional and currently available

3. Evaluation of the scope of work
4. Preparation of initial financial assessment and analysis
5. Consultation with counsel with respect to legal issues and approach
6. Preparation of report and accounting schedules and, if necessary, a document brief
7. Negotiations between parties
8. Assistance to counsel in court
9. Expert evidence in court

The accountant may also be called upon to give a differing opinion than that reached by an equally credible expert accountant on the other side. This may arise due to different interpretations of the facts of the case or various alternate accounting techniques that might be available under the circumstances. In some cases, given equally plausible alternatives, the case is often decided on whichever side has the most credible expert witness.

7.4 PRETESTIMONY ACTIVITIES

Pretestimony activities would generally encompass the preparation of the report of the expert witness to a final stage. Generally, and without stating that the list is all inclusive or appropriate in all circumstances, reports should include a discussion of the following financial aspects:

1. Issues
2. Reliance on data to achieve conclusion
3. Assumptions made in arriving at conclusion
4. Restriction on assumptions
5. Date of information cut off
6. Opinion and conclusion based upon the available documentation
7. Limitations of opinion and sensitivity to assumptions
8. Detailed schedules and documents supporting the opinion and conclusion

One important problem in the preparation of reports and accounting summaries arises from delegation of tasks to junior accountants. If the person giving evidence has not had direct knowledge or has not examined the specific documents or prepared the accounting summaries, it may be possible that the expert will be trapped under the hearsay rule. If tasks are delegated, it is important that the review process entail review of all work to original documentation on a 100 percent basis.

It is also important to know the effect of other assumptions on the conclusion or opinion reached in the report. It is often possible to trap an expert into giving alternate opinions, based upon other assumptions that had not been considered. Generally, working papers supporting the report and accounting schedules should not show contradictory conclusions to the report as they are producible in court. This does not advocate that working papers should be deleted or amended subsequent to preparation; rather, it is a caution that these papers should be prepared with the precept that they could ultimately be submitted to the court and, as such, should take the appropriate form at the time of preparation.

Another aspect of pretrial preparation relates to the availability of all notes that the witness intends to use or rely upon. These notes may be requested in evidence for the court or may be producible during examination.

Further activities could consist of the determination of whether or not sufficient material is present to support the report. It may be necessary to derive information from other witnesses to support the expert's conclusions. This is normally done by reference to discoveries or earlier will-says. Unfortunately, the witness cannot refer to these unless he has direct knowledge of their contents. If the accountant has relied upon opinions or information presented by other witnesses then he must either hear that evidence in court or have the transcript or agreed statement of facts available. Otherwise, that information and any opinions drawn based upon that information would not be allowable.

It is often useful to have a list of all other witnesses including the witnesses of the other side. This is important so that the expert is not surprised by the existence of other experts or reports. Further, one can then determine if it is necessary to be present for the testimony of those witnesses and can obtain the related court approval. If another expert will be present, then it is incumbent upon the expert witness to examine the alternate reports and to assess whether or not reasonable points are brought up by the other side that may affect the credibility of the expert's report.

Other pretestimony activities encompass ensuring that any required graphic displays are ready and available, that all important discussions with the lawyer have been held as part of the pretestimony meetings discussed above, and that the expert has a complete understanding of his report and all other relevant issues in the trial *whether accounting-related or not*. Most important, the expert must ensure that he or she has agreement with counsel as to the sequence of evidence to be presented by the expert and the strategy for presenting it. It is often useful to have a "dry run" at the direct testimony, with all the questions being posed by the counsel to the expert witness in order to avoid surprises during trial.

At pretestimony meetings, it is often appropriate to discuss the qualifications of the witness again to assure that they are current, to discuss the strengths and weaknesses of the case and to discuss and agree as to what parts of the expert's reports, if not all, are to be entered into court as exhibits.

7.5 ON THE STAND: DEMEANOR AND APPEARANCE

As will be appreciated, the appearance of the expert witness often lends itself to an assessment of the credibility of that witness. As such, it is recommended that the witness be well groomed and neatly dressed. In the accountant's case, the expected image is often that of a dark business suit. This appearance may be used to enhance image to psychological advantage. In the witness box, the witness should maintain a poised, alert appearance, stand firmly, and be ready to take the oath. It is important to keep control of hands and to avoid fidgeting, and to maintain eye contact with the questioner while keeping an eye on the judge. As the judge will be taking notes, the witness should speak slowly enough to ensure that the judge does not fall behind. The voice should be strong and directed to the questioner. The witness should enunciate clearly.

Several things should be definitely avoided in giving evidence. These range from drinking five cups of coffee immediately prior to testimony or chewing bubble gum while giving evidence, to small physical mannerisms that may affect your appearance. These physical mannerisms, which might be as simple as rubbing hands together continually, looking down at one's hands, continually moving in the stand, or jingling coins in a pocket, could quickly become irritating to the judge.

7.6 DIRECT EXAMINATION

The purpose of direct examination is to enable counsel for the side you represent to draw out the financial evidence to prove their case. Most likely, this will be only a reiteration of what has been previously discussed with your counsel outside of the courtroom. It is still very important, however, to refresh your memory by reference to anything you may have read, written, or given in evidence on the case beforehand.

Direct examination is the most organized aspect of the trial; it is the stage in which the expert's credibility must be established with the judge or jury. According to the concept of the primary memory feature, people remember best what they hear first and last. This is often a useful idea to employ in giving or structuring evidence. A further noteworthy point is that the jury will often have a limited attention span in a long trial, thus, it is often useful to use a "grab/give/conclude" method of presenting evidence.

To a witness the interpretation of questions and the ability to listen are crucial skills. Even though the witness may have already gone through a mock direct examination, it is critical that each question be carefully evaluated again—the witness should reflect upon the questions asked and not anticipate them (they may have been changed, anyway, since the time of rehearsal). Throughout, one must remember that this aspect of testimony was rehearsed in advance and as such is the easiest aspect of examination.

In answering questions, one must be honest. Less obvious, however, is the need to avoid bias and prejudice in answering. The answers to all questions should be clear and concise and, where complex terms are used, should be clarified. Use of notes should be limited as much as possible in order to maintain eye contact with both the judge and the rest of the court.

Accounting schedules should be described accurately and succinctly in layperson's terms. Schedules are by their nature concise documents and should be described in that manner. If opinions are given, they should be given with conviction once the appropriate groundwork has been laid.

7.7 CROSS-EXAMINATION

Cross-examination is truly the highlight of the adversarial court system in that it is geared to allow counsel to either clarify or make points at the witness's expense. As such it is generally the most difficult part of the trial process for any witness. Anything unexpected can turn up that might refute or embarrass the witness. The witness's credibility is constantly called into question.

The goals of the opposing counsel during cross-examination are threefold. The first goal is to diminish the importance of the expert testimony just presented. The second goal might be to have the expert testify in support of the opposing position by providing a series of assumptions. The third goal is to attack the opinion itself or to show the inadequacies of the expert's work in arriving at his or her opinion, thereby discrediting the opinion, the report, and the witness in the eyes of the court.

The opposing counsel can attack or question anything that has been said or entered into court. This includes notes, working papers, affidavits, will-says, reports, and preliminary trial or discovery transcripts. Often, cross-examination is an atmosphere of confrontation and contradiction. At all times, one must remember that the financial expert witness, however crucial to the case, is merely a piece of the puzzle.

Most importantly, the witness must not take attacks or situations of discredit personally. There are many ways to discredit an expert witness. Throughout the process it is important for the witness to maintain pride and professional integrity. An adage to remember is that "even mud can be worn well."

In general, proper attitude and demeanor during direct examination are also applicable to cross-examination, with the exception that opposing counsel wants to reduce or limit the impact of the witness's evidence—it is natural to feel a certain amount of apprehension at this stage, and this does a great deal to keep the witness alert.

The jury often watches the judge, and therefore the expert can often take a clue as to the tempo and reaction of the jury and the judge to the evidence being presented. Slight changes in style and presentation could be made accordingly.

The opposing counsel usually has a plan of cross-examination in mind, and an expert witness should be able to establish this direction to prevent from falling into a trap or erring. A danger of this, of course, is that the witness will spend as much time planning ahead as answering the questions and as such may not be giving appropriate weight to the immediate questions. Further, in attempting to anticipate, the witness may misunderstand the question.

When being asked questions, the expert should evaluate questions carefully and take time to consider the answer. The witness should be calm and pause before answering, and tread very carefully towards the answer, knowing exactly how it relates to both the question and the issues in front of the court.

In giving an answer it is important to be honest and to avoid the appearance of bias and prejudice. It is also equally important not to exaggerate, ramble in answering, allow one's self to be baited or attempt to be humorous. One of the most devastating blows to a litigation or defendant is when an expert witness makes a transparent attempt to hide errors or loses his or her temper.

Generally, it is often a rule of thumb of the expert witness that free information should not be given away or volunteered. Further, during the answer, it may often be extremely difficult to avoid getting trapped in various assumptions, "what if" scenarios, and generalities presented by counsel during cross-examination. If this occurs, retrench by asking for the question to be rephrased in smaller components.

It is critical never, never to underestimate the accounting expertise of the opposing counsel. Often, opposing counsel will be underplaying their understanding of the issues in order to lull the expert into a sense of security. Obviously, this can lead the expert into a difficult situation.

In general terms, opposing counsel's golden rule is to cross-examine only if the cross-examination would be to the benefit of a case. In asking questions of the witness, opposing counsel will generally ask either short questions in plain words or leading questions. Usually counsel knows the answers to his or her questions in order to eliminate any surprises and to allow him or her to lead the witness along. Several techniques are also available to destroy the witness and yet not touch his evidence.

The opposing counsel will generally evaluate answers and then take a specific approach that furthers its argument. Generally, the witness will not be allowed to explain or elaborate on the question at that time as that would allow the witness to alter the thrust of the carefully orchestrated cross-examination. Opposing counsel is also continually questioning or evaluating how its last question and answer could be used against the witness. If the question has raised new ground, can it be developed and used to enhance the opposing counsel's position.

Opposing counsel will often prepare by reading all earlier testimony and publications of the witness. The opposing counsel might also speak to other lawyers as to the witness's capabilities in court if they have had an experience with the witness. This may indicate specific weaknesses in the witness. If any are discovered, the questioning of the witness will probably be directed to that area.

Opposing counsel may also attempt to take psychological control of a witness by:

1. Use of physical presence to intimidate

2. Nonstop eye contact
3. Challenging space of the witness
4. Fast pace to questions to confuse witness
5. Not allowing the expert to explain or deviate from the exact question

Physical domination is often used by opposing counsel. Opposing counsel will quickly discover the response pattern of the expert and might take an aggressive stance to lead the expert to the point where he or she is unsure, with devastating results.

7.7.1 Strategies Employed in Cross-Examination

The following strategic methods could be employed by opposing counsel to discredit a witness or to diminish the importance of his or her testimony. These methods could be used singly or in conjunction with one another and are not an all-encompassing list. A good counsel in cross-examination will quickly discover the witness's weak areas and employ any possible techniques to achieve his or her goal. Thus, it is often useful to have an overall understanding of some of the more common methods employed.

7.7.1.1 "Myopic Vision". Myopic vision entails getting the expert to admit to excessive time being spent in the investigation of a matter, then selecting an area to highlight of which the expert is unsure or has not done much work. This area may not be central to the issues in the case or in fact be critical but must be relevant to conclusions reached. Then, the opposing counsel will make a large issue of it and prove that the expert's vision is myopic in that the work was limited in extent or scope and, as such, substandard. At the same time, the question of fees could be drawn in to show that large sums were expended to have this "obviously incomplete" work done.

7.7.1.2 "Safety/Good Guy". This approach is often taken by not attacking the expert and hence lulling him or her into a feeling of false security. Then, opposing counsel might find a small hole that could then be enlarged quickly. This approach is often characterized by being friendly and conciliatory, by which the jury is made sympathetic to the cause of the opposing counsel. Opposing counsel may also attempt to achieve a certain amount of association with the witness that will make the witness want to help the opposing counsel in bringing out information in the matter. Doing so may result in the witness giving information that otherwise would not have been given. With this additional information, it may be possible to find a chink or hole in the evidence and develop it further.

7.7.1.3 "Contradiction". Opposing counsel may use leading questions to force the witness into a hard or contradictory position. Alternately, counsel can establish the credibility in court of a potentially contradicting document or quote from other articles written by experts in the field. If these documents or articles are in contradiction to the expert, then an admission can be obtained by the expert as to that contradiction. If the contradiction exists, then the expert might be drawn into an argument as to who is the most appropriate or experienced expert in the circumstances. Instances have also occurred where the witness has contradicted himself or his own article written several years prior merely because of his lack of memory or confusion due to the attack.

7.7.1.4 "New Information". Opposing counsel may introduce new information that the expert might not be aware of and refer to a specific relevance in the conclusions reached by the expert witness. This is normally done in order to institute confusion in the witness's mind in the hopes that the witness might contradict himself or herself or develop a series of alternate scenarios given the new information that would show that his existing report and opinions are no longer of value.

7.7.1.5 "Support Opposing Sides Theory". This approach establishes and recognizes an expert's qualifications and evidence. The same information used by the expert is then used and interpreted by opposing counsel in a different fashion to support an alternate theory. By getting the expert to agree to the alternate interpretation of the facts and the alternate theory, in effect, the opposing counsel has made the expert the witness for the other side. This technique is useful to obtain concessions from the witness that would damage his or her conclusions and, ultimately, his credibility.

7.7.1.6 "Bias". This method draws the expert's counsel and the expert together to show possible collusion as to the evidence being presented in testimony and hence show bias. This can be shown if the opposing counsel can determine that the expert's counsel had instructed the witness as to what to say or by limiting the expert's scope and hence his or her conclusions. This approach can also focus on the question of whether or not the expert was told by his or her client what to do and look for. With this approach, opposing counsel can attempt to show that the expert overlooked important documentation in an effort to assist his or her client.

7.7.1.7 "Confrontation". This very simple method is the continued use of a confrontation of wills to put the witness into a situation where he or she might lose emotional control and demonstrate anger. Once a witness has exploded, credibility normally disappears.

7.7.1.8 "Sounding Board". This method uses the witness as a sounding board to reacquaint the jury with the favorable aspects (to opposing counsel) of the case. This technique often uses the "is it not true" and "would you agree with me" approach. Constant nonstop agreement is useful to browbeat the expert. In the eyes of the judge and jury, agreement with various questions raised by the opposing counsel may also be assumed to be a general concurrence with the position of opposing counsel. This is often a very valuable psychological tool.

7.7.1.9 "Fees". This method attacks the witness on the basis of taking an inordinate amount of time for the result given. Further, the attack may indicate a lack of complete work and may be correlated to the fees charged. This method is often related to "bias" and "myopic vision." Due to the gross amount of fees or reoccurring engagements with a client, it may be suggested that the witness and his opinion are, in fact, bias to retain the client. This technique often builds to a conclusion by which the opposing counsel shows that the work was superficial and unprofessional, yet a great deal of money was received by the expert for this and other areas of service to the client, the direct inference being that the testimony was purchased or that the expert was paid to overlook facts contradictory to the conclusions made.

7.7.1.10 "Terms of Engagement". This technique is normally employed by obtaining the original engagement letter and examining the terms of engagement. Opposing counsel can then show that the expert intended only to look at various items in support of his or her client and glossed over any alternative theories, generally to the detriment of the opposition. As such, the witness could be portrayed as not impartial.

7.7.1.11 "Discrediting the Witness". Discrediting the witness is based upon the concept of proving that the expert is unworthy to be a credible witness instructor to the court. This can often be accomplished by showing that the expert is currently or has previously been grossly biased, prejudiced, corrupt, convicted of criminal activities, shown to engage in immoral activities, made inconsistent statements, acquired a reputation for a lack of veracity, and/or exaggerated his or her qualifications.

Discrediting could also consist of looking at the quality of the expert's educational background to reveal any other unusual activities that might bias the witness or exclude him or her from the court as an expert.

7.8 SURVIVAL TECHNIQUES

There are 10 points for the expert witness to remember in both preparing for and giving evidence at trial. These are:

1. Prepare your material completely
2. Know your material thoroughly
3. Plan your testimony in advance
4. Be alert
5. Listen carefully
6. Carefully consider each answer, and pause before answering
7. Be honest and avoid bias
8. Clarify—use simple words
9. Keep your cool
10. Maintain professional pride and integrity throughout

REFERENCES

1. Michigan Supreme Court Rules of Evidence, Rules 702, 703, 704, 705, 706, 707.
2. Ontario Court of Appeals, Regina v. Scheel, May 12, 1978.
3. Hoyer v. U.S., 8 Cir., 223 F., 2d 134, 1955, p. 138
4. Daniel v. U.S. 5 Cir., 343 F. 2d 785, 1965, Hunter District Judge, p. 789.

8

RULES FOR THE PROSECUTION OF CRIMINAL FRAUD

The essential ingredients of a crime are that it be a voluntary act or omission (*actus reus*) and that it be accompanied by a certain state of mind (*mens rea*). *Mens rea* is often called *evil intent*. Over the years certain acts have been made crimes even without a showing of immorality or evil intention. Such a crime is referred to as *malum prohibitum*, (i.e., a thing that is wrong because it is prohibited by statute, not because it is immoral). *Malum prohibitum* crimes are distinguished from their historical Common Law cousins in that the latter are *malum* in *se*, that is, wrong by their nature, or immoral. Many of the so-called white-collar crimes are violations in the *malum prohibitum* sense— they require no showing of an evil intention. Such crimes as using false weights and measures or false advertising, and other business regulatory violations regarding health and safety, are included in this grouping. Traffic law violations and building code violations also fit into the category. Tax evasion, however, though a *malum prohibitum* type of crime, does require a showing of willfulness or evil intention as an element of the crime.

As is evident, Anglo-American law is not supplied with simple, clean, and clear distinctions or categories. There are many "slopovers" in our legal concepts. The guilty mind, or *mens rea* component, has come to mean "purposely," "knowingly," "recklessly," or "negligently." The criminal act or omission to act is seen as being voluntary if any of those four descriptors can be applied to the act or omission.

The voluntariness of an act is intended to distinguish it from an act committed by mistake or in ignorance of the facts that may not be criminal. Such an act may be viewed as involuntary, as for example, an act committed by a person during an epileptic seizure. But ignorance of the law (not of fact), when a duty to be knowledgeable exists, is no excuse. Certain acts are considered to be recognized as harmful and immoral by any reasonable adult (they are immoral per se). But criminal responsibility cannot be affixed to an act committed by a person who suffers from mental disease or mental defect. Other mitigating circumstances include self-defense and defense of one's property.

One further distinction needs to be addressed here. In criminal cases, guilt must be established beyond a reasonable doubt. That burden of proof is on the prosecution and relates to the notion that an accused is presumed to be innocent until proven guilty. In civil cases the burden of proof is on the plaintiff and is discharged when the plaintiff's proofs are convincing by a "preponderance of the evidence," (i.e., by less proof than that required in a criminal case).

The burden of proof remains with the prosecution throughout a criminal trial. It never shifts to the accused. If the state does not meet its burden of proof by making a *prima facie* case (providing the minimum of proofs that can legally sustain a conviction), the defendant may request a directed verdict of acquittal. If a *prima facie* case is made, then the burden of going forward with the evidence shifts to the defendant. If he or she fails to introduce such proofs as will create a reasonable doubt as to guilt, the defendant may stand convicted.

8.1 RULES OF CRIMINAL PROCEDURE

Courts have found it expedient to propound rules of evidence and procedure for the orderly, efficient, and fair conduct of investigations and trials, so that truth may be properly and logically ascertained. We therefore now have rules of criminal procedure and rules of evidence. These rules dictate both the proper conduct of criminal investigations and the proper conduct of criminal trials.

Rules of criminal procedure deal with the methods of apprehending, charging, and trying suspects; the imposition of penalties upon conviction; and the methods for challenging the legality of conviction after judgment is entered. The process begins with the investigative phase by police authorities. The police are to comport themselves according to certain dictates while an allegation of a criminal act is being investigated—by not abridging the constitutional rights of a suspect, by not resorting to unnecessary force in apprehending a suspect, and by gathering evidence in such a manner that its value is not legally jeopardized or compromised.

During the investigative phase evidence is gathered of the material elements of the crime (the *corpus delicti*); that is, that a specific crime was in fact committed, and that in all probability it was committed by a specific person or persons because competent, relevant, and material evidence exists of their involvement.

That information is then referred to a prosecuting authority who reviews the facts and available evidence and decides whether they are suitable and adequate to justify a conviction. If so, a formal accusation is made in the form of an indictment or information—usually an indictment for a felony charge and an information for a misdemeanor, in federal cases. But private citizens may also initiate a formal accusation by filing a complaint with an officer of the court or, in some jurisdictions, an officer of the law.

Trials are generally held in the legal jurisdiction in which the crime was committed. A public trial, by jury if so desired by the defendant, is usually accorded in criminal cases in the United States. A defendant also has the right to testify on his or her own behalf. But a decision not to testify cannot be held against a defendant, because the burden of proof is on the prosecution and a defendant cannot be forced to testify against himself or herself.

The rules of criminal procedures deal mainly with such general areas as:

1. Search and seizure
2. Arrest
3. Interrogation and confessions
4. Pretrial identification procedures
5. Right to counsel

The body of case law that has developed over these procedural issues is prodigious. It is beyond the intention of the authors to probe into these matters extensively. Suffice it to say that our discussion is scarcely more than an overview.

Search-and-seizure procedures by police authorities are circumscribed in the United States by the constitutional guarantee of the Fourth Amendment, which reads as follows:

Amendment IV (1791)

The right of the people to be secure in their persons, houses, papers, and effects, against unreasonable searches and seizures, shall not be violated, and no warrants shall issue, but upon probable cause, supported by Oath or affirmation, and particularly describing the place to be searched, and the persons or things to be seized.[1]

The Fourth Amendment (indeed the first 10 Amendments, the Bill of Rights) was intended to constrain the powers of the federal government over its subjects. Later construction and interpretations by the United States Supreme Court applied the constraints of the first 10 amendments to state governments as well; using as its vehicle the Fourteenth Amendment, which reads as follows:

Amendment XIV (1868)

Section 1. All persons born or naturalized in the United States, and subject to the jurisdiction thereof, are citizens of the United States and of the State wherein they reside. No State shall make or enforce any law which shall abridge the privileges or immunities of citizens of the United States; nor shall any State deprive any person of life, liberty, or property without due process of law; nor deny to any person within its jurisdiction the equal protection of the laws.[2]

Searches and seizures that violate the Fourth Amendment result in the exclusion of the evidence so gathered at criminal trials; even if the evidence is otherwise relevant, material and competent. So a "reasonable" search conducted with a warrant based on probable cause, supported by oath or affirmation, and describing with particularity the place to be searched and the persons or things to be seized, is the proper course for the police to follow if they do not wish to compromise a criminal case with tainted evidence.

The other constitutional amendments that bear on the present discussion are the Fifth and Sixth Amendments. They appear as follows:

Amendment V (1791)

No person shall be held to answer for a capital, or otherwise infamous crime, unless on a presentment of indictment of a Grand Jury, except in cases arising in the land or naval forces, or in the Militia, when in actual service in time of War or public danger; nor shall any person be subject for the same offense to be twice put in jeopardy of life or limb; nor shall he be compelled in any criminal case to be a witness against himself, nor be deprived of life, liberty, or property, without due process of law; nor shall private property be taken for public use, without just compensation.[3]

Amendment VI (1791)

In all criminal prosecutions the accused shall enjoy the right to a speedy and public trial, by an impartial jury of the State and district wherein the crime shall have been committed, which district shall have been previously ascertained by law, and to be informed of the nature and cause of the accusation; to be confronted with the witnesses against him; to have compulsory process for obtaining witnesses in his favor, and to have the Assistance of Counsel for his defense.[4]

8.2 RULES OF EVIDENCE

A court trial is intended to deduce the truth of a given proposition. In a criminal case the proposition is the guilt or innocence of an accused person. The evidence introduced and received by the court to prove the charge must be beyond a reasonable doubt—not necessarily to a moral certainty—by the quantity and quality of evidence that would convince an honest and reasonable lay person that the defendant is guilty after all the evidence is considered and weighed impartially.

But what is evidence and how can it be weighed and introduced? In a broad sense evidence is anything perceptible by the five senses and any form of species of proof such as testimony of witnesses, records, documents, facts, data, or concrete objects, legally presented at a trial to prove a contention and induce a belief in the minds of the court or jury. In weighing evidence the court or jury may consider such things as the demeanor of a witness, his bias for or against an accused, and any relationship to the accused. Thus evidence can be testimonial, circumstantial, demonstrative, inferential, and even theoretical when given by a qualified expert. Evidence is simply anything that proves or disproves any matter in question.

To be *legally* acceptable as evidence, however, testimony, documents, objects, or facts must be competent, relevant, and material to the issues being litigated, and be gathered in a lawful manner. Otherwise on motion by the opposite side the evidence may be excluded. Now perhaps we should elaborate on relevancy, materiality, and competency: Relevancy of evidence does not depend upon the conclusiveness of the testimony offered, but upon its legitimate tendency to establish a controverted fact.[5]

Some of the evidentiary matters considered relevant and therefore admissible are:

1. The motive for the crime
2. The ability of the defendant to commit the crime
3. The opportunity to commit the crime
4. Threats or expressions of ill will by the accused
5. The means of committing the offense (possession of a weapon, tool, or skills used in committing the crime)
6. Physical evidence at the scene linking the accused to the crime
7. The suspect's conduct and comments at the time of arrest
8. The attempt to conceal identity
9. The attempt to destroy evidence
10. Valid confessions

The materiality rule requires that evidence must have an important value to a case or prove a point in issue. Unimportant details only extend the period of time for trial. Accordingly a trial court judge may rule against the introduction of evidence that is repetitive or additive (that merely proves the same point in another way), or evidence that tends to be remote even though relevant. Materiality then is the degree of relevancy. The court cannot become preoccupied with trifles or unnecessary details. For example, the physical presence of a suspect in the computer room or tape library or near a terminal on a day in which a spurious transaction was generated may be relevant and material. One's physical presence in a non-computer-related area of the building may be relevant, but immaterial.

Competency of evidence means that which is adequately sufficient, reliable, and relevant to the case and presented by a qualified and capable (and sane) witness—the presence of those characteristics, or the absence of those disabilities that render a witness legally fit and qualified to give testimony in a court applied in the same sense to documents or other forms of written evidence. But competency differs from credibility. Competency is a question that arises before considering the evidence given by a witness; credibility is one's veracity. Competency is for the judge to determine; credibility is for the jury to decide.

The competency rule also dictates that conclusions or opinions of a nonexpert witness on matters that require technical expertise be excluded. For example, testimony on the cause of death by an investigating officer may not be appropriate or competent in a trial for murder or wrongful death, because one is not qualified by education, study, and experience to make such an assessment. Testifying that there were "no visible signs of life" when the body was found may be acceptable, however.

When an expert witness is called upon to testify, a foundation must be laid before testimony is accepted or allowed. Laying a foundation means the witness's expertise must be established before a professional opinion in rendered. Qualifying a witness as an expert means demonstrating to the judge's satisfaction that by formal education, advanced study, and experience the witness is knowledgeable about the topic upon which his or her testimony will bear. The testimony of experts is an exception to the hearsay rule.

The hearsay rule is based on the theory that testimony that merely repeats what some other person said should not be admitted because of the possibility of distortion or misunderstanding. Furthermore, the person who made the actual statement is unavailable for cross-examination and has not been sworn in as a witness. Generally speaking, witnesses can testify only to those things of which they have personal and direct knowledge, not give conclusions or opinions.

But there are occasions—exceptions—when hearsay evidence is admissible. Some examples:

1. Dying declarations, either verbal or written
2. Valid confessions
3. Tacit admissions
4. Public records that do not require an opinion but that speak for themselves
5. *Res gestae* statements—spontaneous explanations, if spoken as part of the criminal act or immediately following the commission of such criminal act
6. Former testimony given under oath
7. Business entries made in the normal course of doing business

Photocopies of original business documents and other writings and printed matter are often made to preserve evidence. These are used by investigators so that original records needed to run a business are not removed and to ensure that in the event of an inadvertent destruction of such originals a certified true copy of the document is still available as proof. The certified copy may also be used by investigators to document their case reports. At the trial, however, the original document—if still available—is the "best evidence" and must be presented. The best evidence in this context means primary evidence, not secondary; original as distinguished from substitutionary; the highest evidence of which the nature of the case is susceptible: "A written instrument is itself always regarded as the primary or best possible evidence of its existence and contents; a copy, or the recollection of a witness, would be secondary evidence."[6] Further, "Contents of a document must be proved by producing the document itself."[7]

8.3 ELABORATION ON HEARSAY EXCEPTIONS

In an idealistic sense, a court trial is a quest to determine the truth. However, the means of acquiring evidence are clearly variable. Some means are legal, others are illegal; for example, they may violate constitutional guarantees against unreasonable search and seizure, forced confessions, or failure to be represented by counsel. Realistically, therefore, a court trial can result only in a measure of truth and not in absolute truth in the philosophical sense.

Yet in the Anglo-American tradition, witnesses, other than experts, cannot generally testify as to probabilities, opinions, assumptions, impressions, generalizations, or conclusions, but only as to things, people, and events they have seen, felt, tasted, smelled, or heard firsthand. And even those things must be legally and logically relevant. Logical relevancy means that the evidence being offered must tend to prove or disprove a fact of consequence. But even if logically relevant, a court may exclude evidence if it is likely to inflame or confuse a jury or consume too much time. And testimony as to the statistical probability of guilt is considered too prejudicial and unreliable to be accepted.

Testimony as to the character and reputation of an accused may be admissible under certain conditions, even though it would seem to violate the hearsay rule. Such testimony may be admitted when character is an element of the action; that is, when the mental condition or legal competency of the accused is in question.

Evidence of other crimes committed by an accused is not generally admissible to prove character. It may be admitted for other purposes, however, such as proof of motive, opportunity, or intent to commit an act.

The credibility of a witness may also be attacked by a showing that he or she was convicted of a serious crime (punishable by death or imprisonment for more than a year) or for such crimes as theft, dishonesty, or false statement. Such conviction should have occurred in recent years—usually within the last 10 years.

Evidence can be direct or circumstantial. Direct evidence proves a fact directly; if the evidence is believed, the fact is established. Circumstantial evidence proves the desired fact indirectly and depends on the strength of the inferences raised by the evidence. For example, a letter properly addressed, stamped, and mailed is assumed (inferred) to have been received by the addressee. Testimony that a letter was so addressed, stamped, and mailed raises an inference that it was received. The inference may be rebutted by testimony that it was not in fact received.

The "best evidence" rule deals with written documents proffered as evidence. The rule requires that the original if available, and not a copy thereof be presented at a trial. If the original has been destroyed or is in the hands of an opposite party and not subject to legal process by search warrant or subpoena, then an authenticated copy may be substituted. Business records and documents kept in the ordinary course of business may be presented as evidence, too, even though the person who made the entries or prepared the documents is unavailable.

8.4 OTHER PERTINENT RULES OF EVIDENCE

8.4.1 Chain of Custody

When evidence in the form of document or object (means or instrument) is seized at a crime scene, or as a result of subpoena *duces tecum* (for documents), or discovered in the course of audit and investigation, it should be marked, identified, inventoried, and preserved to maintain it in its original condition and to establish a clear chain of custody until it is introduced at the trial. If gaps in possession or custody occur, the evidence may be challenged at the trial on the theory that the writing or object introduced may not be the original or is not in its original condition and therefore is of doubtful authenticity.

In order that a seized document may be admissible as evidence, it is necessary to prove that it is the same document that was seized, and that it is in the same condition as it was when seized. Because several persons may handle it in the interval between seizure and the trial of the case, it should be adequately marked at the time of seizure for later identification, and its custody must be shown from that time until it is introduced in court.

An investigator or auditor who seizes or secures documents should quickly identify them by some marking, so they can later testify that they are the documents seized and that they are in the same condition as they were when seized. The investigator might, for instance, write his or her initials and the date of seizure on the margin, in a corner, or at some other inconspicuous place on the front or back of each document. If circumstances suggest that such marking might render the document subject to attack on the grounds that it has been defaced or it is not in the same condition as when seized, the investigator or auditor can, after making a copy for comparison or for use as an exhibit to the report, put the document into an envelope, write a description and any other identifying information on the front of the envelope, and seal the envelope.

These techniques should be applied any time the investigator or auditor comes into possession of an original document that might be used as evidence in a trial. If an auditor makes a copy of documentary evidence, he or she should take steps to preserve the copy's authenticity in case it is needed as secondary evidence if the original document is not available for the trial.

8.4.2 Secondary Evidence

To introduce secondary evidence, one must explain satisfactorily the absence of the original document to the court. Secondary evidence is not restricted to photocopies of the document; it may consist of testimony of witnesses or transcripts of the document's contents. Whereas the federal courts give no preference to the type of secondary evidence, the majority of other jurisdictions do. Under the majority rule, testimony (*parol evidence*) will not be allowed to prove the contents of a document if there is secondary documentary evidence available to prove its contents. However, before secondary evidence of the original document may be introduced, the party offering the contents of the substitute must have used all reasonable and diligent means to obtain the original. Again, this is a matter to be determined by the court.

When the original document has been destroyed by the party attempting to prove its contents, secondary evidence will be admitted if the destruction was in the ordinary course of business, or by mistake, or even intentionally, provided it was not done for any fraudulent purpose.

8.4.3 Privileged Communications

The rule supporting privileged communications is based on the belief that it is necessary to maintain the confidentiality of certain communications. It covers only those communications that are a unique product of the protected relationship. The basic reason behind these protected communications is the belief that the protection of certain relationships is more important to society than the possible harm resulting from the loss of such evidence. Legal jurisdictions vary as to what communications are protected. Some of the more prevalent privileged relationships are:

1. Attorney–client
2. Husband–wife
3. Physician–patient
4. Priest–penitent
5. Law enforcement officer–informant

When dealing with privileged communications, the following basic principles should be considered:

1. Only the holder of a privilege, or someone authorized by the holder, can assert the privilege.
2. If the holder fails to assert it after having notice and an opportunity to assert it, the privilege is waived.
3. The privilege may also be waived if the holder discloses a significant part of the communication to a party not within the protected relationship.

4. The communication, to be within the privilege, must be sufficiently related to the relationship protected (for example, communications between an attorney and client must be related to legal consultation).

It should be noted that under common law a person cannot testify against his or her spouse in a criminal trial. While married, neither may waive this testimonial incompetency. This witness incompetency must be distinguished from the confidential communications between spouses made and completed during the marriage, which retain the privileged status after the marriage has ceased.

Conversations in the known presence of third parties do not fall within the purview of communications. The protected communications are those that are in fact confidential or induced by the marriage or other relationship. Ordinary conversations relating to matters not deemed to be confidential are not within the purview of the privilege.

The laws of different states vary widely in the application of the principles of privileged communications. Depending on what protected relationship is involved, different rules may apply regarding what communications are protected, the methods of waiver, and the duration of the privilege.

Whenever an auditor/investigator is confronted with the need to use evidence in the nature of communications between parties in one of these relationships, he or she should consult with an attorney, especially if the evidence is crucial to the case.

8.5 ADMISSIONS AND CONFESSIONS

Criminal phenomena occur as a result of four factors:

1. Motivations of criminals

2. Opportunities to commit crimes, presented by weaknesses in people, internal controls, safeguards, or protection measures

3. Means to commit crimes—resources (knowledge of weaknesses), skill in exploiting them, and a mental disposition to do so (confederates and tools)

4. Methods—plans to execute crimes with the least chances for discovery and identification

Crime is a risk for both victim and victimizer. The victim's risk is the loss of something valuable—life, limb, or property. The victimizer's risk is the loss of freedom, social status, and possibly of life, limb, and property, too. But criminals intend to gain something as a result of a crime, something to which they are not legally entitled. So a criminal, a rational one, at least, has to concern himself or herself with weighing the risk of discovery, apprehension, and conviction against the intended gain.

If the risk of discovery and the amount of the gain are great, then more time and thought must be spent on planning, on disguising, on surprise, on escape, and possibly on covering up the crime. Fortunately for police authorities, criminals tend to act in haste. Their plans often go awry. They do not anticipate everything that can happen. So they usually add to their arsenal of defenses rationalizations for their misconduct, or alibis. "It wasn't me; I was elsewhere." "The devil made me do it." "I am poor and misunderstood, a victim of oppression." "He [the victim] had it coming." "I must have been crazy for doing what I did."

These rationalizations are what police interrogations are intended to sort through. Here again, intuition may play an important role. Criminals usually offer an excuse or justification for what they do. Sometimes they feign ignorance or illness. Sometimes they even feign amnesia. Interrogation cuts through these defenses, excuses, and rationalizations.

During an interrogation it is important to remain sensitive not only to what the suspect is saying but to the manner in which it is being said, and to observe facial expressions, body and eye movements, word choices, and posture. Verbal fencing with the suspect, a la Perry Mason conducting a cross-examination, does not help. Challenging the suspect's comments on the basis of pure logic and rationality does not persuade most criminals to confess. Suspects can stay with a lame excuse forever and almost come to believe it after a while. The reason they persist in lying is that their crimes were not committed out of a sense of logic but mainly for emotional reasons such as lust, greed, anger, or envy. So in interrogating suspects, one must be prepared to deal with their emotions. "Why did you do it?" is not a very good question early on. It calls for intellectualizing by the suspect, or rationalizing, a much more common response to that type of question.

A better choice are questions that do not get to the *gravamen* (main issue) of the crime at all—questions about a suspect's feelings and emotions:

1. How are you feeling?

2. Can I get anything for you?

3. Do you feel like talking?

4. Can I call anyone for you?

The purpose of these innocuous questions is to build rapport, first on the emotional level and then later on a rational level. Not all criminal suspects feel compelled to talk about their crimes, but most do, if one establishes rapport with them. And rapport can be established even after advising them of their right to remain silent.

An apprehended suspect or one merely being informally interviewed before arrest is under great emotional strain. Fears of conviction and incarceration are exacerbated. These fears must be realized before intelligent conversation can be achieved. The tone and demeanor of the interrogator/interviewer must be reassuring, if not friendly. Intuition enters this process only if the investigator remains calm, dispassionate, and sensitive to the emotional needs and concerns of the suspect or witness. Intuition does not work when one's mind is cluttered with isolated facts or a listing of questions to pose about the details of a crime.

Once an investigator has learned something about the suspect's history, family, friends, and feelings, he or she can then discern the most appropriate interrogation technique. If the suspect remains cold, aloof, and noncommunicative while innocuous questions are posed, he or she will get about the same when the questions get more serious. One will need a command of all the known facts of the crime to gain a confession in that case.

If the suspect responds openly to the investigator's offers of kindness and civility, the latter can lead by general questioning. The investigator will let the suspect resolve the crime and not get in the way by verbal bantering, accusation, or sparring. One should let the suspect tell the story in his or her own way, even if one knows some of the facts are being distorted. One can always come back and ask for clarification, and can then compare the conflicts with the testimony of witnesses or confederates.

The importance of confessions and admissions to the resolution of crime should not be understated. Without such confessions and admissions, many crimes would never be solved. In some fraud cases, accounting books and records do not provide enough evidence to convict a suspect. So a confession from a thief, defrauder, or embezzler makes these fraud prosecutions easier. A freely given confession often details the scheme, the accounts manipulated and the uses to which the purloined funds were applied. The evidence gathered after a confession may corroborate the crime. A confession alone will not support a criminal conviction, however, so the auditor will have to retrieve from the data available within the accounting system and from third-party sources enough corroborating evidence to support the confession.

REFERENCES

1. Fourth Amendment, 1791
2. Fourteenth Amendment, 1868, Sec. 1
3. Fifth Amendment, 1791
4. Sixth Amendment, 1791
5. ICC v. Baird, 24 S. C.T. 563, 194, U.S. 25, 48 L. Ed. 860
6. Manhattan Malting Co. v. Swetland, 14 Mont. 269, 36, p. 84
7. Nunan v. Timberlake, 85 F. 2d 407, 66 App. D.C. 150

PART THREE

ISSUES RELATED TO THE AUDITOR AND FRAUD INVESTIGATOR

9

THE EXPECTATION GAP

Financial auditors (internal and external) are still in doubt as to the extent of their legal and professional responsibility for fraud detection when conducting routine financial audits. But courts do not seem to be of a similar mind. Nor does the investing public. There is a growing public perception that auditors by the nature of their education, intuition, and work experience can sniff out fraud wherever and whenever it exists in books of account. That standard is far higher than anyone in the audit professions has ever advocated. In fact, the public's perception of auditor responsibility for fraud detection is highly unrealistic. No auditor could ever afford to relax in the face of such a strict standard of care. Nor could any auditor afford the premiums for professional liability insurance if the public's perception of the standard became a legal reality. What then *is* the fraud auditor's legal standard of care, and what is his or her responsibility for detecting fraud?

9.1 ARE AUDITORS LIABLE FOR FRAUD DETECTION?

One source for insight on the external auditor's standard of care and responsibility for fraud detection is *American Jurisprudence*.[1] Under the general heading "Accountants" that volume offers this:

> It is generally recognized that a public accountant may be held liable on principles of negligence, to one with whom he is in privity, or with whom he has

a direct contractual relation, for damages which naturally and proximately result from his failure to employ the degree of knowledge, skill, and judgment usually possessed by members of that profession in the particular locality.

But Section 17, page 366, reads as follows:

An accountant is not an insurer of the effectiveness of his audit to discover the defalcations of frauds of employees but may be found liable for fraudulent or negligent failure to discover such defalcations because of lack of compliance with proper accounting procedures and accepted accounting practices or by his contract in the light of circumstances of the particular case. . . . And the employer may be precluded from recovery because of his own negligence when it has contributed to the accountant's failure to perform his contract and to report the truth.

The second excerpt gives auditors a breather. Obviously external auditors should not be held liable for not detecting fraud when their clients deceive them.

In 1984 the Institute of Internal Auditors issued its Statement on Internal Auditing Standards, which deals with deterrence, detection, investigation, and reporting of fraud.[2] The Standard makes a number of interesting points in its Foreword and Summary. To quote from the Foreword:

Fraud is a significant and sensitive management concern. This concern has grown dramatically in recent years due to a substantial increase in the number and the size of the fraud uncovered. The tremendous expansion in the use of computers and the amount of publicity accorded computer-related frauds intensifies this concern. The issue of the internal auditor's responsibilities for deterrence, detection, investigation, and reporting on fraud has been a matter of much debate and controversy. Some of the controversy can be attributed to the vast differences in internal auditing's charter from country to country and from organization to organization. Another cause of the controversy may be unrealistic—nevertheless increasing—expectations of the internal auditor's ability to deter and/or detect fraud in some circumstances.

Generally Accepted Accounting Standards (GAAS), as promulgated by the American Institute of Certified Public Accountants (AICPA), assign the "independent auditor. . .the responsibility, within the inherent limitations of the audit process, to plan his or her examination to search for errors or irregularities that would have a material effect on financial statements."[3] It would seem by that statement that external auditors are not liable for detecting immateri-

fraud. The cost of attempting to do so could become enormous in corporations like IBM, GM, AT&T, and Exxon. And even though the external auditor is duty bound to evaluate internal controls, management may override such controls.

But in *United States v. Arthur Young & Co.* (March 21, 1984)[4] the Supreme Court tried to define *professionalism* in the accounting profession in the loftiest terms. In a unanimous decision the Court stated:

> By clarifying the public reports that collectively depict a corporation's financial status, the independent auditor assumes a *public* responsibility *transcending any employment relationship* with the client. The independent public accountant performing his special function *owes ultimate allegiance to the corporation's creditors and stockholders*, as well as to the investing public. This "public watchdog" function demands that the accountant maintain *total independence from the client at all times* and requires *complete fidelity to the public trust*. To insulate from disclosure a certified public accountant's interpretations of the client's financial statements would be to ignore the significance of the accountant's role as a *disinterested analyst charged with public obligations*. [*Emphasis added*]

The Court continued:

> It is therefore not enough that financial statements *be* accurate; the public must also perceive them as being accurate. *Public faith* in the reliability of a corporation's financial statement depends upon the *public perception* of the outside auditor as an independent professional. [*Emphasis added*]

The Auditing Standards division of the AICPA summarized auditor's responsibilities regarding fraud and illegal acts under current GAAS in the July 1985 newsletter *In Our Opinion*, as follows:[5]

> The auditor's responsibility to detect and report fraud is set out in Statement on Auditing Standards (SAS) No. 16, The Auditor's Responsibility for the Detection of Errors or Irregularities, (1977) and SAS No. 17, Illegal Acts by Clients, (1977). The standards were developed as a direct result of problems in the business community in the mid-1970s. The disclosure of client frauds, such as Equity Funding, and questionable payments, primarily in foreign countries, stirred the profession to adopt more specific standards in the area of client misconduct.

SAS No. 16 establishes an affirmative requirement for auditors; the auditor is required to plan the examination to search for material errors and irregularities and to carry out the search with due skill and care. The auditor's responsibility with regard to illegal acts is less distinct; because auditors are not lawyers trained to recognize illegal acts, they are not expected to search for illegal acts, but rather to be aware that some matters that come to their attention during the examination might suggest that illegal acts have occurred. If the auditor discovers an error, irregularity, or illegal act, he is required to report it to management, and depending on its significance, possibly to the Board of Directors or its Audit Committee. The auditor is also required to assess the effect on the financial statements and, if material, to insist on adjustment or additional disclosure in the statements or to qualify the audit report.

Auditors recognize that although there is an affirmative responsibility to search for material errors and irregularities, there is a chance that they will not be found. The auditor tests selectively, that is, accounts are usually sampled rather than examined 100 percent. Thus if the sample does not identify a fraudulent transaction, the auditor will be less likely to suspect one in the unsampled portion of the financial statements. Auditors, of course, control this sampling risk, but to eliminate it would require auditors to examine all of the entity's transactions for the year which would result in astronomical audit costs, and this still would not necessarily detect cleverly forged or unrecorded transactions.

The public furor in North America about the liability of external auditors for detection of fraud is not yet over. In fact the pressure for imposing more stringent requirements on public accountants for the detection of fraud appears to grow with each passing day. In Canada, the Canadian Institute of Chartered Accountants (CICA) has established a Commission to examine this issue. In the United States, the introduction of the Financial Fraud Detection and Disclosure Act of 1986 is a manifestation of the public's concern. The congressional history and details of that bill[6] follow:

Background

The regulatory system established by the federal security laws is based upon the concept of complete and fair disclosure of important information to investors and other users of corporate financial reports. This regulatory system is administered by federal agencies, such as the Securities and Exchange Commission [SEC] working in concert with private, independent auditor firms which check corporate financial records and certify the reports given to the public. Over the past several years, numerous cases of massive financial fraud have occurred where the independent auditors either failed to detect or to report the fraudulent activities at the companies being audited. These include E.F. Hutton, United American Bank, General Dynamics, E.S.M. Government Securities, Inc., Home State Savings and Loan of Ohio, American Savings and Loan of Florida, Saxon Industries, San Marino Savings and Loan of California, and many others. The costs of these frauds have been enormous both financially and in terms of public confidence in the soundness of the nation's economic system. The American Institute of Certified Public Accountants (AICPA), a private trade organization, establishes the generally accepted auditing standards (GAAS) which are used by independent auditors and accepted by the SEC. Under present GAAS rules independent auditors do not include significant procedures to detect management fraud as part of their audit, and their consideration of fraud is restricted to its material impact on a corporation's financial statements. For a large corporation financial fraud amounting to millions or even hundreds of millions [of dollars] could go unreported because such amounts would not be considered material to the total financial condition of the corporation.

Even when actual fraud and illegal acts are discovered, the GAAS rules only say that the auditor should inform the company's management and consider resigning from the audit account. There is no requirement that auditors report fraud or illegal acts to the appropriate government authorities. In addition auditors rely on the internal control systems of a corporation, but do not issue an opinion regarding the adequacy of management's internal controls. Thus financial fraud has occurred in many corporations which have been allowed to operate with substandard or nonexistent internal controls because the independent auditor did not report on the adequacy of internal controls.

The AICPA and the SEC were criticized on this issue 10 years ago by the Senate Subcommittee on Reports, Accounting and Management. That Subcommittee's final unanimous report stated that auditors should look for illegal acts and report them to government authorities. The AICPA appointed its own study group, the Cohen Commission, which failed to recommend active detection and reporting of illegal acts. The SEC and the AICPA did nothing further until the Subcommittee on Oversight and Investigations began its accounting hearings on February 20, 1986.

At the March 6, 1985, hearing Chairman Dingell was joined by other members in expressing his concern about an audit rule which merely suggested that the auditor, as the public watchdog, only consider leaving the premises if he found a criminal, instead of reporting the criminal to the proper authorities. In response, the AICPA established a new group, the Treadway Commission, to further study the issue. Neither private accounting organizations nor the SEC have the authority to grant independent auditors immunity from legal action which could arise as a result of their fraud detection and disclosure responsibilities, so legislation is the only way to fully protect auditors performing their duties in good faith.

Chairman William Seidman of the Federal Deposit Insurance Corporation who formerly headed a large audit firm, agreed with Chairman Dingall and Congressman Wyden at the Subcommittee's April 28, 1986, hearing that auditors should look for fraud and report it to regulators.

Legislative Proposal

The Financial Fraud Detection and Disclosure Act of 1986 (the Act) amends the federal securities laws to provide reasonable assurance that fraudulent activities at companies covered by these laws will be discovered and reported to the proper authorities. The Act will not apply to small businesses or other companies which are exempt from the securities laws. The Act is necessary now because the SEC and the accounting profession lack the authority to provide full legal protection for auditors who report fraudulent activities.

The Act strengthens the present regulatory system of federal agencies working with private audit firms by establishing clear standards for the detection and reporting of financial fraud, as well as the tools necessary to meet those standards and fully protect auditors performing their duties. The Act does not create a new federal agency or regulatory burden, but instead assures that audits conducted under the present system will meet the legitimate concerns of Congress and the public that major companies are not operating fraudulently. The incremental audit costs of meeting the standards established by the Act are miniscule when compared with the lost billions of dollars resulting from frauds and the decline of public confidence in the integrity of the nation's economic system. The Act has several basic provisions as described below:

(1) The Act requires that auditors include specific and substantive procedures for detecting financial fraud as part of the audit plan. Present audit standards regard fraud detection as incidental to the financial audit. Therefore many auditors either fail to recognize indications of fraudulent activities, or else convince themselves that such activities are not within the scope of the audit and that the auditor has no responsibility to act on such matters.

(2) The Act requires that auditors evaluate the internal control systems established by corporate managers in order for the auditor to determine whether those internal controls assure that corporate assets are being handled properly and lawfully. Present audit standards on reviewing internal controls are not strong enough in this regard.

(3) The Act requires auditors to issue a written report that: (a) gives the auditor's opinion regarding the adequacy of internal control systems; (b) identifies any weaknesses in those systems; and (c) states that the audit was conducted in a manner which provides reasonable assurance that fraudulent activities have been detected and reported.

The auditor's written report is the place where the auditor gives opinions on the results of the audit. Present standards do not require that the auditor issue an opinion on fraud detection or the adequacy of internal controls.

(4) The Act requires that the individuals actually responsible for the audit sign the audit opinion on behalf of the firm conducting the audit. Present audit opinions only bear the name of the audit firm conducting the audit, even though the firms auditing most SEC registrants are giant organizations with hundreds of partners and thousands of staff. This provision in the Act is a no-cost, common sense way to enhance personal accountability to help assure that the audit was conducted properly. It also provides personal recognition for the individuals doing good work, and enables the public and regulatory authorities to determine if auditors identified with problem audits are being made responsible for other audit engagements. The practice of individuals signing work product personally on behalf of their firm is commonplace in the legal profession and others.

(5) The Act requires public disclosure of known or suspected fraudulent activities, and gives the auditor a responsibility for assuring such disclosure. Present standards do not provide adequate disclosure of fraudulent activities, and auditors have no responsibility for assuring disclosure. Under existing rules the corporate managers who are often involved in the fraud are given sole responsibility for reporting to the public. The Act requires disclosure of activities that, in the auditor's view, may be fraudulent so that users of financial reports and corporate managers will be able to take appropriate actions without the delay inherent in complete legal proceedings to reach conclusions which satisfy every requirement of law and evidence. In most cases losses are magnified and irrevocable by the time legal proceedings are completed. This provision meets the requirement of the securities laws to give fair and complete disclosure of important information to the public in a timely manner, so that the financial markets will operate efficiently.

(6) The Act requires that auditors report known or suspected illegal activities to the appropriate government, regulatory, or enforcement authorities. Present standards only require that auditors report such activities to corporate management (who may be involved), and then consider resigning the audit engagement if the corporate managers do not take appropriate action. Auditors are employed to be the public watchdog, and the public is not served by the present standard, which only suggests that the watchdog leave the premises if he finds a criminal. This provision also improves the efficiency of government regulatory and enforcement authorities by giving them the information which can only be found through the work of on-site auditors.

(7) Finally, the Act provides complete legal protection for auditors who perform their duties under the Act in good faith. Although the public expects auditors to report known or suspected fraudulent activities, auditors could suffer legal liability for honest reporting of their findings. This provision is consistent with the legal protection given to officials acting in good faith on the public's

behalf in other areas. While the Act establishes clear standards to meet the public's expectations of auditors, it also protects the men and women who will implement its provisions.

Authorities in business management insist that the audit function, both internal and external, is a visible deterrent to fraud and accounting irregularities. This pious assumption is predicated on a theory held by police authorities who suggest that the visible presence of a uniformed police officer or marked police car on regular patrol deters crime. Since the passage of the Foreign Corrupt Practices Act in 1977, many corporations have established internal and EDP audit functions or bolstered the staffs of these organizational units only to discover that there was no decrease in the number of defalcations—frauds, thefts, and embezzlements—by corporate users. In "Perception of the Internal and External Auditor as a Deterrent to Corporate Irregularities," Wilfred C. Uecker, Arthur P. Brief, and William R. Kinney, Jr., tested the hypothesis that an increase in the perceived aggressiveness by internal and external auditors in detecting corporate irregularities would function as a deterrent.[7] The study concludes that managers contemplating acts of management fraud are not deterred by the presence of internal and external auditors; neither does an increase in the perceived aggressiveness of the internal or external auditor significantly decrease the occurrence of corporate irregularities.

So one may have to make one's own case for a viable fraud reduction strategy. Should it be:

1. More and better laws?
2. More and better auditors and auditing?
3. More and better audit training?
4. More and better internal controls?
5. More honest senior managers?
6. All of the above?

9.2 FRAUD DETECTION AND DISCLOSURE: ARE NEW TEETH NEEDED?

On June 23, 1986, John Shad, Chairman of the Securities and Exchange Commission, in testimony before the House Subcommittee on Oversight and

Investigations, made the following apologies for the nation's financial reporting system (i.e., the U.S. Congress, the SEC, and the accounting profession):[8]

1. The evidence concerning alleged audit failures suggests that the system is working well.

2. There are 11,000 publicly owned companies that file reports and registration statements with the SEC.

3. During the past three years the SEC has taken action against 100 issuers or their employees for disclosure violations. In 43 other cases the SEC has taken action against public accountants for "alleged misconduct".

As Chairman Shad explains:

"The Commission's primary concern of course is with fraud that materially impacts the public financial reports of registrants. While the Commission has been unable (and it is unaware of any study that has been able) to quantify the nature and impact of such fraud, it is clear that fraudulent accounting or disclosure practices, however isolated, can cause substantial harm to investors, creditors, and others."

To add emphasis to Chairman Shad's concerns, we make note of the recent collapse of E.S.M. Government Securities. That celebrated fraud shook the world's confidence in the United States banking system. When news of the enormity of the E.S.M. debacle (the waiting lines of depositors in Ohio) reached the world media, gold prices jumped $30 an ounce, and the American dollar plummeted on international money markets.

The significance and long-term impact of the E.S.M. case is not unlike the Three Mile Island nuclear disaster. Should another untoward event occur anywhere in the world (such as the Chernobyl nuclear plant in Russia), faith in the present system may be lost forever. Likewise, the ripple effects of E.S.M. will be felt for many years to come. Trust in the financial system has been severely damaged by fraud.

This is no longer the time for damage assessment and control. This is the time for risk reduction and risk prevention. There are obvious and serious risks and perils out there. At least 95 cases exist of public companies and regulated financial institutions in the United States in which stockholders, creditors, or regulatory authorities alleged that audit failures by major public accounting firms occurred during the past 15 years.

REFERENCES

1. *American Jurisprudence*, 2d ed., Vol. 1, Sec. 15, Rochester, NY: The Lawyers Cooperative Publishing Co., 1962, pp. 365–366.

2. *Statement of Internal Auditing Standards*, Institute of Internal Auditors, 1984.

3. "Generally Accepted Accounting Standards,"*AICPA Professional Standards*, Vol. 1, AV Sec. 327, New York: American Institute of Certified Public Accountants, pp. 322–323.

4. U.S. v. Arthur Young & Co., 465-U.S. 805, 104 S. Ct. 1495, 79L, Ed. (2d) 826

5. *In Our Opinion*, July 1985, Vol. 1, No. 2.

6. Financial Fraud Detection and Disclosure Act, H.R. Doc. No. 4886, 99th Cong. 2d Sess.

7. Wilfred C. Uecker, Arthur P. Brief, and William R. Kinney, Jr., "Perception of the Internal and External Auditor as a Deterrent to Corporate Irregularities," *The Accounting Review*, (July 1981), pp. 465–478.

8. John Shad, (June 23, 1986), Chairman of Securities and Exchange Commission, testimony before House Subcommittee on Oversight and Investigations.

10

ACCOUNTING: FOR NONACCOUNTANTS

10.1 THE DOUBLE-ENTRY BOOKKEEPING SYSTEM

Accounting became a quasiscience about 500 years ago in Italy when a man named Pacioli invented the concept of double-entry bookkeeping. In double-entry bookkeeping each business transaction has two corresponding parts of equal amounts, one called a *debit*, the other a corresponding *credit*. If a merchant sells an article for $100 and takes in cash, for example, the business entry is a debit to the Cash account of $100 and a credit to Sales for $100. This process was an improvement over the single-entry method in which nothing but cash coming in or cash going out was recorded. Pacioli's method provided the merchant with a more detailed breakdown of his business operations and was a forerunner of what we now call a management information system. It told the merchant what his total sales were by day, month, or year. It told him what his cash receipts were for the day, week, month, or year, and therefore what was available for the payment of bills from his suppliers of merchandise. When he paid his suppliers, the entry made on his books was a debit to Purchases and a credit to Cash.

This combination of controls over income and outgo then provided the merchant with a simple way to calculate his profit or loss from business. For example, if he bought an article of merchandise for $50 and sold it for $100, his record-keeping system would disclose that he had a gross profit of $50 on that particular sale. The many sales made in the course of a business day were totaled at the end of the day. Against those sales a number of purchases were also made; these, too, were totaled. Then, by offsetting the sales against the purchases, the merchant would know whether the day's business resulted in a gain or reduction in cash. For example:

Total Sales for the Day	$500
Total Purchases for the Day	250
Cash Gain	$250

Total Sales for the Day	$500
Total Purchases for the Day	750
Cash Loss	($250)

But daily accountings like the above were not totally accurate. All items purchased that day were not necessarily intended to be sold that day. (A merchant normally does not sell out his whole inventory every day and start anew the next morning.) Some method had to be developed to account for merchandise left on hand at the end of the business day. So a formula was derived to determine what the true amount of profit was on a day's sales. That amount was called *cost of sales*. Cost of sales was determined by the following formula:

Beginning Inventory + Purchases − Ending Inventory = Cost of Sales

Profit could then be determined as follows:

Total Sales for the Day		$500
Beginning Inventory	200	
Purchases	+250	
	$ 450	
Ending Inventory	−200	
Cost of Sales		−250
Gross Profit		$ 250

But gross profit did not tell the whole story. Cost of sales was not the only cost incurred in doing business; other expenses also had to be deducted to determine whether a profit had been made. For example, the store rent had to be allocated against that day's sales as well as expenses such as heat, store help, advertising, taxes, interest, and depreciation of store equipment.

Assuming the store was open 20 days per month and monthly rent was $200, each day's sales should be offset by a charge of $10 for rent ($200 ÷ 20 days).

A recast of the merchants profit-and-loss statement for the day might therefore resemble the following:

STATEMENT OF INCOME

Sales		$500
Cost of Sales		−250
Gross Profit		$250
Less Other Expenses:		
Rent	$10	
Heat	5	
Labor	50	
Advertising	5	
Taxes	10	
Interest	3	
Depreciation	2	
Total Other Expenses		−85
Net Profit		$165

Double-entry bookkeeping was therefore intended to give the merchant a more accurate method to calculate his profit and make business decisions about the future (e.g., when or whether to expand, or to add new items of merchandise to sell, or to discontinue items that did not sell well or had less profit potential).

But double-entry bookkeeping had another virtue as well. The merchant could determine at any point in time what his business was worth. This formula was derived by totaling all his assets (what he owned) and then subtracting all his liabilities (what he owed). This was called a *balance sheet*. The balance sheet for the merchant might look like this:

BALANCE SHEET

Assets:

Cash on Hand	250
Inventory	200
Store Equipment	1,000
	$1,450

Liabilities:

Accounts Payable: Trade	100
Accrued Expenses Payable	85
	185
Proprietor's Equity:	1,265
	$1,450

Still another benefit of double-entry bookkeeping was the ability it provided to take what accountants called *trial balances* as a measure to test the accuracy of entries made in the accounting records. If all entries are composed of corresponding debits and credits of equal amounts, tabulating the balances in all accounts should come up with identical totals for both debits and credits. This is what bookkeepers, accountants, and auditors call *balancing the books*. If the totals of all debit and credit balances do not agree, it is a sign of mathematical error in the entry of transactions in journals or postings to ledger accounts.

Journals are called *books of original entry*. They contain details of each transaction of the business. Journals come in a number of varieties, such as sales journals (Exhibit 10.1), purchases journals (Exhibit 10.2), cash receipts journals (Exhibit 10.3) and cash disbursements journals (Exhibit 10.4). Journals are used to record daily transactions of a business as these transactions are made. Journals are summarized at some point in time, usually monthly, and the summary totals, by specific account categories, are then posted to general ledger accounts from which the financial statements are prepared (Exhibit 10.5).

DATE 1987	CUSTOMER NAME	ACCOUNTS RECEIVABLE DR.	SALES CR.
Jan. 3	ABC Company	$ 100 √ √	$ 100
Jan. 4	XYZ Company	400 √ √	400
Jan. 5	Smith Company	600 √ √	600
Jan. 6	Jones Company	300 √ √	300
Jan. 7	PQR Company	200 √ √	200
		$1,600 √	$1,600 √

√ = Posted to General Ledger Account
√√ = Posted to Accounts Receivable Subsidiary Ledger

EXHIBIT 10.1. Sales journal.

DATE 1987	VENDOR NAME	PURCHASES DR.	ACCOUNTS PAYABLE CR.
Jan. 3	A Wholesaler	$ 100	$ 100 √ √
Jan. 4	B Wholesaler	200	200 √ √
Jan. 5	C Wholesaler	300	300 √ √
Jan. 6	D Wholesaler	400	400 √ √
Jan. 7	E Wholesaler	500	500 √ √
		$1,500	$1,500

√ = Posted to General Ledger Account
√√ = Posted to Accounts Payable Subsidiary Ledger

EXHIBIT 10.2. Purchases journal.

The subsidiary ledgers specified for accounts receivable and accounts payable are books that are organized by customer and vendor name and show each individual transaction with that customer or vendor. The accounts receivable subsidiary ledger (Exhibit 10.6) details each sale to each customer, usually by date and invoice number and by amount of the sale. The accounts payable subsidiary ledger (Exhibit 10.7) details each purchase from each vendor, usually by date, vendor invoice number, and amounts of purchase. In some accounting systems the purchase order number may also be indexed as a further measure of control. Exhibits 10.1−10.7

DATE 1987	CUSTOMER NAME	CASH DR.	ACCOUNTS RECEIVABLE CR.
Jan. 3	ABC Company	$1,000	$1,000 √ √
Jan. 4	XYZ Company	500	500 √ √
Jan. 5	Smith Company	400	400 √ √
Jan. 6	Jones & Company	600	600 √ √
Jan. 7	PQR Company	2,000	2,000 √ √
		$4,500 √	$4,500 √

√ = Posted to General Ledger Account
√√ = Posted to Accounts Receivable Subsidiary Ledger

EXHIBIT 10.3. Cash receipts journal.

DATE 1987	VENDOR NAME	CASH CR.	ACCOUNTS PAYABLE DR.
Jan. 3	A Wholesaler	$ 500	$ 500 √ √
Jan. 4	B Wholesaler	100	100 √ √
Jan. 5	C Wholesaler	50	50 √ √
Jan. 6	D Wholesaler	200	200 √ √
Jan. 7	E Wholesaler	300	300 √ √
		$1,150 √	$1,150 √

√ = Posted to General Ledger Account
√√ = Posted to Accounts Payable Subsidiary Ledger

EXHIBIT 10.4. Cash disbursements journal.

10.2 THE ROLE OF AUDITING IN THE ACCOUNTING SYSTEM

Exhibits 10.1 through 10.6 are examples of bookkeeping and accounting. Auditing is something else again. Auditing is the process of reviewing and testing accounting systems, records, reports, policies, and procedures to determine whether they are adequate for the purpose intended by management and adequate in terms of standards established by auditing authorities. The process of auditing entails the testing—usually on a sampling basis— of a

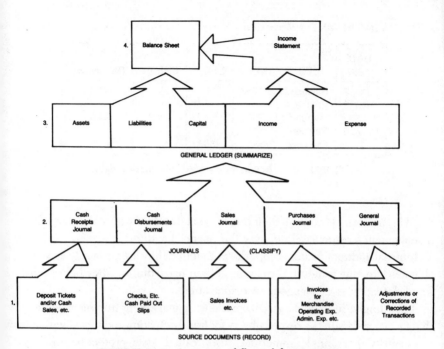

EXHIBIT 10.5. Anatomy of financial statements.

CUSTOMER NAME: ABC Company

DATE 1987	DESCRIPTION	DEBIT	CREDIT	BALANCE
Jan. 2	Balance from 1983			$1,200
Jan. 3	Sale: Inv. #1203	$100		$1,300
Jan. 3	Payment Received		$1,000	$ 300

EXHIBIT 10.6. Accounts receivable subsidiary ledger.

sufficient number of accounting transactions, procedures, and practices to assess their adequacy. Adequacy means reliability, accuracy, timeliness, completeness, and validity (i.e., freedom from major errors and omissions—but not necessarily freedom from fraud).

Fraud detection (or discernment) is not the usual purpose of a financial audit. Financial auditors are not responsible for discovering or uncovering

VENDOR NAME: A Wholesaler

DATE 1987	DESCRIPTION	DEBIT	CREDIT	BALANCE
Jan. 2	Balance from 1983			$400
Jan. 3	Purchase Invoice #17–307		$200	$600
Jan. 3	Payment— Our check #2533	$500		$100

EXHIBIT 10.7. Accounts payable subsidiary ledger.

fraud in the normal course of their duties. That duty falls within the purview of management's responsibilities, say the financial auditors.

Internal auditors do not accept the notion that they are primarily accountable for detecting frauds in the course of their usual duties. They believe that fraud detection is a management responsibility.

Accordingly, in many large corporations, management (top management, that is) may delegate the responsibility for fraud detection and investigation to its security personnel, sometimes now called asset-protection or loss-prevention specialists, many of whom have no accounting or auditing skills; therefore, detection of financial frauds tends to fall between the cracks. It never gets done on a regular, routine, or systematic basis. When information or complaint of a fraud surfaces, the security people may be called in and then teamed with internal or external audit resources to conduct the necessary investigation. The audit function in large corporations (either internal or external) is intended to deter or discourage fraud more than it is to detect fraud.

Accounting systems operate within the framework of various accounting cycles; of them, the most common to all businesses are the revenue cycle and payments cycle.

10.3 THE REVENUE CYCLE

The revenue cycle includes all systems that record the sale of goods and services, grant credit to customers, and receive and record customer remittances. (See Exhibit 10.8)

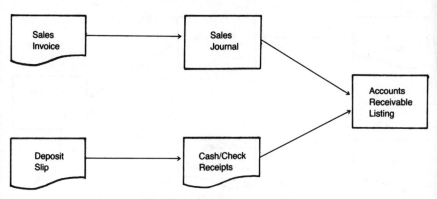

EXHIBIT 10.8. Revenue cycle.

The details of a product sold for a price, or of professional services rendered for a fee, are set out in a document called a *sales invoice*. Details of the sales invoice are listed in the sales journal. When payment is made by the customer, the company records the payment on a deposit slip that is ultimately listed in the cash receipts journal.

Business organizations also keep a list of those customers who owe money. This listing, produced by comparing the sales journal and the cash receipts journal, is called *accounts receivable*. It is usually prepared monthly and shows, for each customer listed, the age of the receivable (i.e., whether the customer has owed the company for 30, 60, 90, or more than 90 days).

Thus the system of sales, receipts, and receivables constitutes the revenue cycle of any company. The primary documents are the sales invoice (evidence of the sale to the customer) and the deposit slip (evidence of payment by the customer to the company). The best evidence of payment is the customer's canceled check, which is returned directly to the customer's bank for processing.

10.4 THE PAYMENTS CYCLE

The payments cycle includes all systems that record the acquisition of goods and services for use in the business exchange for payment or promises to pay. Exhibit 10.9 charts this cycle.

In order to produce its product for sale a company incurs various types of

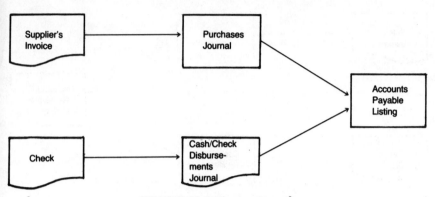

EXHIBIT 10.9. Payments cycle.

expenditures. These include the acquisition of land, buildings, and equipment; purchase of materials and supplies; and payments to the employees of the company.

Purchases are made from many different suppliers. A supplier's invoice is evidence of a transaction. This invoice is sent to the company and sets out the details of the transaction. The company lists certain details of the supplier's invoice in the purchase journal.

If the company has the funds available the supplier is usually paid within 30 days. This payment is evidenced by the company's canceled check. All checks are recorded in the company's check disbursements journal when they are issued. This journal is simply a listing of the checks that have been paid to the various suppliers and other creditors and individuals doing business with the company.

Most companies attempt to keep track of what they owe to suppliers. This is usually done on a monthly basis. The company prepared an accounts payable listing by comparing what is recorded in the purchases journal and what is recorded as paid in the check disbursements journal. This listing may detail how long they have owed various suppliers (for example: 30, 60, or 90 days).

10.5 BANK RECONCILIATION

The monies received by the company (as recorded in the cash receipts journal) and the monies paid out by the company (as recorded in the check disbursements journal), are processed through the bank account of the company. In order to ensure that the transactions recorded in these journals agree with those transactions shown on the bank statement, a monthly bank account reconciliation is prepared. Exhibit 10.10 charts this process.

10.6 THE GENERAL LEDGER

Over the course of a year many transactions are listed in each of the four journals. If these lists were added only annually, the room for error would be enormous, so businesses total the listing in each journal monthly. These totals are entered into the general ledger.

The general ledger contains a separate ledger sheet for each of the accounts set out in the four journals. If one were to look at an individual sheet in the general ledger, one would expect to find, over a year, up to one entry a month for each account. The monthly entry would be added to the accumulated total, so the total for the year-to-date activity is readily apparent.

Errors do occur within the books of account. To correct these errors an entry is made in the general journal. This journal is kept for the specific purpose of adjusting the general ledger to make necessary changes, including the correction of errors. These entries should set out an explanation for the correction. A general journal entry has the effect of taking an amount from one account, say ABC, reducing the total in the ABC account and transferring that same amount to the other account, XYZ, and increasing the total in XYZ. In this manner the general ledger balances are corrected. Once the correcting or

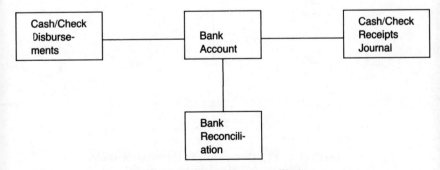

EXHIBIT 10.10. Bank reconciliation.

adjusting entries have been completed, the general ledger then serves as the basis for the preparation of financial statements. Exhibits 10.11 and 10.12 illustrate the components and end product of the general ledger.

10.7 OTHER CORPORATE RECORDS

Other significant documents maintained by the company are the corporate minute book and stockholder records. In many cases these documents are in the possession of the corporate attorney. These documents set out minutes of the meetings of both shareholders and directors of the company as well as details of the share certificates. The ownership of the company is set out as reflected on the certificates.

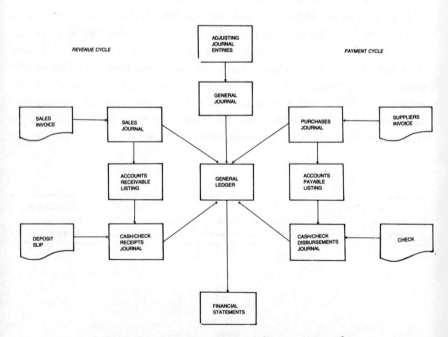

EXHIBIT 10.11. Documents in the revenue cycle.

10.8 COMPUTERIZED ACCOUNTING SYSTEMS

Essentially there are three major elements in a computerized accounting system: (1) key personnel, such as data input clerks, systems analysts, programmers, and librarians; (2) computer hardware (i.e., the physical equipment that includes the central processing unit and such "peripheral" devices as keyboards, printers, and video screens; and (3) computer software (i.e., the programs or instructions that enable the computer to manipulate the data input by the personnel).

These three elements are discussed below. It is important to note that these elements are over and above those found in conventional (noncomputerized) accounting systems, and the normal procedures should still be in place. The major differences are that fewer personnel are directly connected with the actual manipulation of data and instead of people producing reports, the computer produces the report.

Operation of a typical, centralized computer system such as a system using a mainframe or a minicomputer for corporatewide purposes is shown in a simplified flowchart in Exhibit 10.13.

10.8.1 Key Personnel

Most large organizations have a central information-processing department servicing the entire organization. The people employed in that department are computer specialists. They run the mainframe computer or minicomputer as well as maintaining systems for the benefit of the people in other departments (i.e., the systems users). This section briefly describes the jobs in the central computer department:

Systems Analyst—The systems analyst works with the various user departments to determine how their needs can best be met: what data must be entered, what processing must be carried out on the input data, what output must be produced, and with what frequency. The analyst also determines what equipment is necessary to meet the users' needs and how much memory and storage capacity will be needed.

Programmer—The programmer carries on from the criteria developed by the systems analyst. He or she writes, debugs, and installs new computer

PRIMARY DOCUMENT	INFORMATION	EXAMPLE	
SUPPLIER'S INVOICE:	date of preparation name of supplier description of product purchased	supplier's invoice	

	quantity of product
	    purchased
	cost per unit
	total cost possibly with
	    sales tax
		purchase journal	PURCHASES JOURNAL

	address indicating where product delivered	supplier's statement	
	HOW FILED alphabetically by supplier		
CANCELED CHECK:	date of preparation name of payee amount of payment	canceled check	CHECK DISBURSEMENTS JOURNAL

	name and account
	    number of check
	signing authority
	endorsement
	bank stamp indicating
	    location and date
	    negotiated by payee
	preprinted number on
	    check
	description as to type of
	    payment
		check disbursement journal	

	HOW FILED
	numerical sequence by
	    month with bank
	    statement		

GENERAL LEDGER →			

	PRIMARY DOCUMENT	INFORMATION	EXAMPLE
SALES JOURNAL	SALES INVOICE:	date of preparation name of customer description of product sold quantity of product sold price per unit total price (sales value) possibility with sales tax preprinted number on invoice	sales invoice sales journal
		HOW FILED alphabetically by customer numerically by preprinted number	
CASH RECEIPTS JOURNAL	DEPOSIT SLIP:	date of preparation whether cash or check sometimes payor is named bank stamp indicates date deposited indicates if cash withdrawn at time of deposit	deposit slip cash receipts journal
		HOW FILED chronologically by date	
	CUSTOMER CHECK:	primary source document to prepare deposit slip, as the check is eventually returned to customer	

EXHIBIT 10.12. Documents in the payment cycle.

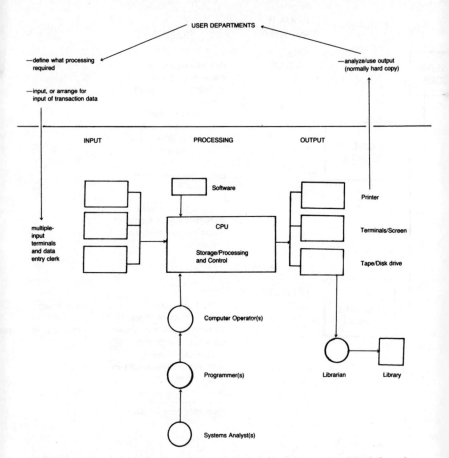

EXHIBIT 10.13. Typically centralized computer system: a simplified flowchart.

programs based on various specifications and the systems design prepared by the systems analyst. The programmer is expected to document new programs in detail and to update the documentation when programs are changed. He or she is also on call in the event of software malfunctioning.

Computer Operator—The computer operator directs the execution of various mechanical tasks by means of a console terminal. The operator schedules tasks for completion by the computer and is responsible for the proper use of input and output devices. The operator usually maintains a computer-usage log recording whose programs were being run and where and when the output was produced.

Data Entry Clerk—The data entry clerk enters all the data, which is then processed directly by the computer. The data can be accumulated and input in large batches or as transactions take place.

Librarian—The librarian stores and retrieves programs and data, usually at a site away from the computer site. Programs and data are normally stored on magnetic tape or disk and serves as a backup if the original software or transaction files are destroyed. The librarian also maintains, under normal circumstances, a log of borrowings from the library.

Decentralized Operators—In addition to their central corporate computer, many organizations now have a network of terminals linked to it. The terminals may be linked via a local area network (i.e., the terminals and the mainframe are in the same building or a nearby building). This link between the terminals and the central computer may be achieved through ordinary telephone lines, or via satellite, microwave, or some other means if the terminals and the central computer are remote.

With a network in place, the need for a data-entry operator in the central department may disappear. Instead, operators using terminals or local area networks or at remote sites can enter data directly into the central computer. Clearly, this decentralized system of processing increases computer systems' vulnerability because more people have access to the computer under conditions that may be less easily controlled. Passwords and other methods of restricting access have to be relied on heavily to prevent people from tampering with programs and files.

10.8.2 Computer Hardware

Computer equipment may be on-line or off-line. An on-line system permits the operator to access and manipulate information in the computer, changing the data base immediately and receiving information from the computer immediately. In contrast, off-line systems involve an intermediate step of some kind before processing takes place.

Generally, computer hardware includes (1) equipment for preparing data for processing, (2) input devices, (3) central processing unit, (4) auxiliary storage devices, and (5) output devices.

Data Preparation Equipment—This equipment is used to convert the data into a machine-readable format. Depending on the method of inputting the information into the computer, numerous devices could be employed. These devices include magnetic tape, optical character readers, and paper-punch tape. Increasingly, preparatory stages are being bypassed altogether, and data is entered directly into the computer via on-line terminals.

Input Devices—Input equipment includes such components as keyboards and video screens that show what is being entered, display instructions, and formats for inputting. Some screens respond to touch. Pointing devices (called "mice") can also be used with some microcomputers. Computers are already available that will respond to a limited range of voice commands.

Central Processing Unit—The CPU is the heart of the computer; it contains a series of operating programs and a translator that converts data into machine language (binary) on which the CPU itself operates. It stores programmed instructions and data; reads, writes, and moves data and instructions; interprets and performs programmed tasks; and synchronizes all of these activities.

Auxiliary Storage Devices—In addition to its main memory, computers need auxiliary memory to store large volumes of data. The storage equipment holds either magnetic tape or magnetic disks. Stored data is extremely vulnerable to abuse, so methods of storing data are explained in more detail later.

Output Devices—Output equipment includes printers, console typewriters, video display screens, and plotters. The technology of output as well as input devices is constantly being improved, because these devices constitute the interface between human beings and computers.

10.8.3 Computer Software

Software is the generic name for computer programs and their documentation. A program is a set of instructions that directs the computer to perform a task. Software is divided into two main classes: operating software and application software.

Operating software consists of the programs that keep the computer running as automatically as possible. They do not actually process anything (processing is the job of the application's software), but they monitor and perform operations that keep the computer system running.

Applications software consists of computer programs that apply the computer to the user's needs by carrying out a task the user wants performed (processing a payroll, for example). The normal sequence of instructions in an application program is as follows:

1. Read the information entered
2. Process it (add, subtract)
3. Update existing files in the computer's memory with new information
4. Output the new information by displaying, printing, or storing it (or all three).

10.9 MICROCOMPUTERS

Microcomputers have all the components already described. They differ from large mainframe computers and minicomputers chiefly in size, performance, and price. Their performance limitations are being overcome rapidly, and their small size has many advantages—many are transportable (lap-sized models are truly portable), and they can fit comfortably on users' desks. They are also less expensive than mainframe computers. (However, the price of microcomputers systems can be close to that of microcomputers, depending on the system chosen.)

The means used to store computer data are vulnerable to abuse and misuse. The earlier computers often used punched cards to input programs and data. Each punched card represented a line of command and numbers depending on where the punch occurred on the card. It was possible to alter information by taping over the punched holes or by punching additional holes in strategic places. Because of the huge volume of punched cards, one card could easily be removed from or added to the deck without the user knowing that the data had been tampered with.

10.9.1 Paper Tape

At the same time, 8-channel paper tape was being used. This paper tape employed a series of round holes punched in six to eight lines or channels. The machine read their location. The paper tape permitted information to be stored and entered into the computer more easily than punched cards. Although information could not be readily changed on these paper tapes, the tapes themselves were quite fragile.

10.9.2 Magnetic Tape

Magnetic tape is still in use today, but disks, both floppy and hard, are increasingly being used. Information is stored on a disk in the same manner as on the magnetic tape. The disk itself resembles a magnetically coated record album. It has a series of concentric channels that encode the information. The major advantage of disks is that the computer can directly access information anywhere on the disk with great speed. In contrast, a magnetic tape must be read sequentially in order to find the relevant data or instructions.

The density of these disks determines the amount of information that can be stored on them.

Floppy disks or diskettes store information on removable, flexible diskettes. Many microcomputers now have hard disks, a more recent development. Hard disks can store much more information than floppy disks. They are generally not removable, being mounted permanently in the computer's disk drive. Removable hard disks are becoming available.

Floppy disks, being small and light, are easy to steal. When left lying about on desks they present a tempting target. Their surfaces are easily damaged and the magnetic dots can be obliterated by careless handling. Hard disks, on the other hand, are much less vulnerable because they are protected by being housed within the computer's disk drive. Nevertheless the data on both types of disks can be tampered with.

10.9.3 Paper and Microfilm

Data may be stored in hard-copy form such as paper or microfilm. Hard copies show the result of data manipulation or processing by the computer but not necessarily the transactions that occurred in arriving at the output. Paper is a familiar and stable medium but is bulky to store; as a result, more companies are using microfilm as the medium for storing records. Computerized records can be microfilmed directly from the disk or tape.

10.10 FINANCIAL STATEMENT REPORTING

The purpose of preparing financial statements is to report to the owners, the shareholders, or other investors the financial position of a company at a specific point in time and the results of operations for a specified period of time. Statements are usually prepared annually; however, many companies prepare them more often—monthly or quarterly, for example.

Financial statements usually include: (1) a report from the accountant/auditor, (2) a balance sheet, (3) an income statement, (4) a statement of changes in financial position, and (5) notes to financial statements.

10.10.1 Balance Sheet

Current assets are those assets that are realizable into cash within one year of the date of the financial statements. The assets are listed in order of liquidity as follows:

1. Cash
2. Accounts and notes receivable—generally required to disclose separately amounts owing from customers; amounts owing by officers, directors, and shareholders; and amounts owing from affiliated companies
3. Inventory—includes cost of raw material, work in progress, and finished goods. The basis of valuation must be disclosed
4. Prepaid expenses—includes items such as insurance and property taxes that are paid in advance

Noncurrent assets are those assets that are of a fixed or permanent nature.

1. Long-term investments—in common shares of other companies and in the bonds and preferred shares of other companies
2. Fixed assets—includes buildings, land, and equipment on the basis of

their historical cost. The basis of valuation must be disclosed. Fixed assets are reduced by an adequate allowance for depreciation. The basis for depreciating assets must be disclosed

Current liabilities include those items payable within one year of the date of the financial statements. The liabilities are listed in the order in which they are due:

1. Accounts payable and accrued liabilities—includes amounts due to suppliers and governmental agencies
2. Notes/mortgages payable—includes current portion of long-term debt due within one year. Amounts owing to officers, directors, and shareholders and amount owing to affiliated companies must be disclosed separately

Long-term liabilities are those liabilities that are not due within one year, such as bonds, debentures, and similar securities. Particulars as to interest rates, maturity dates, and principal repayments must be given. The balance sheet must disclose notice of default in the payment of principal.

The *shareholders' equity* section of the balance sheet includes:

1. Disclosure of the authorized and issued share capital, namely the number of shares for each class of capital stock, the par value, the dividend rates, the redemption price, and commission provisions, if any
2. The contributed surplus, which represents amounts paid into the company by its shareholders or others in excess of the capital stock issued
3. The retained earnings, which represent the accumulated balance of earnings arising from the operation of the business after payment of dividends. If this accumulated balance is a negative figure, the balance amount is called a deficit, (i.e., the company has lost money from its operations)

10.10.2 Statement of Income

The income statement should present fairly the results of operations for a period of time, usually a year, and should disclose at the minimum the following items:

1. Revenue—total sales of net of discounts, sales tax, returns, and amortization of leasehold improvements; the amount charged for amortization of intangible assets; interest expense; and provision for income taxes

2. Extraordinary items—nonrecurring gains or losses resulting from business activity

APPENDIX I

GENERAL CRITERIA AND STANDARDS FOR EVALUATING AN EXPERT'S QUALIFICATIONS*

A determination that a given person is sufficiently knowledgeable and capable to serve as an expert will depend on two factors. First, does the candidate possess the objective qualifications for the job? Does he or she possess the appropriate credentials, relevant prior experience, and critical information having a bearing on successful resolution of the case?

Second, does the expert, though sufficiently qualified, display the personal characteristics that allow him or her to effectively function as part of the investigative team? Is the individual a team player? Does his or her professional reputation and the quality of previous work recommend usage in the case at hand? Can the expert explain technical complexities in such a way that the criminal justice practitioners, investigators, prosecutors, judges, as well as laymen, the jury, can clearly understand their meaning and importance? Does the expert project a professional manner? Can he or she build and keep rapport with others? The following sections address in detail both the requisite formal credentials and the essential personal characteristics which effective consultants and expert witnesses must display.

Computer Crime Expert Witness Manual, (C) 1980, Koba Associates, Inc. Reprinted with permission of the Bureau of Justice Statistics, U.S. Department of Justice.

CREDENTIALS

Credentials and standards for assessing the knowledgeability of out-of-court experts will vary depending on the area of expertise. Even with regard to laying the foundation at trial for a witness's acceptance by the court as an expert, the criteria, though generally standardized between fields of expertise in the eyes of the law, are not inflexible and are subject to some variation. With these caveats in mind, there are several broad areas in which experts are expected to display credentials and qualifications which distinguish them from the laymen. These include the following:

1. Professional licensure, certification, or registration by a recognized professional body in the field of expertise in question
2. Relevant undergraduate, graduate, and post-graduate academic degrees directly in the field of expertise or a suitable background to it
3. Specialized training and/or continuing professional education beyond academic degrees that indicate up-to-date familiarity with the latest technical developments in the expert's subject area
4. The expert's writings and publications that display technical opinions and are available as part of the general body of knowledge in the subject area
5. Relevant teaching, lecturing and/or other consultancies undertaken by the expert which indicate that he or she is held in high professional esteem in the given subject area
6. Professional associations with which the expert is affiliated
7. Directly relevant prior experience which the expert has gained through undertaking similar assignments, whether as technical advisor or expert witness, in the given subject area
8. Special status, or access to privileged information, peculiar to the case at hand which renders the individual an expert because he or she is in possession of unique facts

Professional Licensure, Certification, or Registration

Most professionals, to some degree regulate their members and feature mechanisms for reviewing a practitioner's qualifications—often at periodic intervals. Endorsements as to competence—a license to practice the profession, a certification in a specialty area, or registration at a central authority in the jurisdiction for purposes of regulating the profession are all common practices. The presence of a professional license, certification, or registration is an important factor in assessing the level of basic competence for technical advisors in most areas of expertise useful in financial and computer-related crime investigations (with the general exception of persons in the victim's employ, or who interfaced with the victim's operations, and are experts because they are in possession of unique facts). Establishing that an individual possesses a license or certification in his or her profession, and/or is registered in the jurisdiction as a practitioner of that profession, is a standard step in laying the foundation at trial for the court to accept the testimony of such an individual as expert.

Determining what standards are used to qualify a practitioner in a given profession can easily be determined by inquiring of the professional licensing or certifying body in question. In addition many jurisdictions require practitioners of a wide variety of professions, and who may have acquired their credentials elsewhere, to register with a central government authority if they desire to practice their profession locally. The central registering authority can be a useful source of information on professional licensing standards locally and perhaps a source of expert referrals.

Many of the more traditional professionals supply experts in crime cases. Those include lawyers, engineers, forensic chemists. Most states have laws on the books that dictate the criteria for professional licensing in these broader professions. (However, qualifications for many of the new computer technology fields have not yet been a subject of state government regulation.)

Academic Degrees

The presence of appropriate academic degrees has traditionally been a key indicator of whether an individual will qualify as an expert witness.[1] Even where an expert is being utilized in a computer-related crime case as a behind-the-scenes technical advisor at the investigative or pretrial stage, the fact he or she may be a "potential expert witness," or that the nature of their employment retention, *qua* consultant, is discoverable by the defense, the presence or absence of academic credentials will be a relevant consideration when assessing overall utility and credibility of an expert.

Generally speaking, the requisite academic degrees for each profession and the identities of those institutions of higher learning whose degree programs are accredited are key facets of state or local licensure, certification, or registration laws or regulations. State or local laws should be consulted on this point.

Despite the strategic importance of appropriate academic credentials for experts whose credibility may be challenged by the defense, with regard to the more technological aspects of the problem, overreliance on academic credentials for experts in computer-related crime cases must be cautioned against. Many universities do not have well developed courses, especially postgraduate, in this area. In addition technological advances are occurring so rapidly that many educational programs are not current. Knowledgeable sources agree fairly consistently that an expert's academic preparation for his discipline should certainly be weighed and considered very carefully, but of equal importance can be how recently the degree was taken and what other continuing education courses have been taken along the way.

Training and Continuing Education Experience

Technological developments in computer programming, electronics, and telecommunications engineering, EDP auditing, computer security, and other specializations are increasing rapidly. Courses of training and continuing education in these areas, as in topical areas such as combatting white-collar crime, economic crime, and computer crime, are being widely offered. Certificates of completion and other objective indicators of ungraded skills as a result of attendance at such courses are frequently offered by professional associations and regulatory bodies.

How many current, relevant training courses and continuing education courses have been attended by the prospective technical expert? How up to date is he or she on the state of the art in this technical field? A showing of such currency is generally a corollary to the presentation of academic credentials to the court at the time an expert witness's qualifications are reviewed. The absence of such current educational updates can be expected not only to impact on the quality of expert advice given to the government but can lead to impeachment of the government's expert witness on cross-examination and to the challenging of the technical accuracy of aspects of the government's case when the identities and qualifications of behind-the-scenes technical advisors relied on when preparing the case are discoverable.

Writings and Publications

Whether a prospective expert witness has published in the field of his or her purported expertise is traditionally an important factor to be reviewed when laying the foundation at trial for the technical advisor to take the stand as an expert witness. Prior publications may be of less relevance when the expert is used as a technical advisor to the investigative or prosecutive team during the case preparation stages. However this is not necessarily the case. The prior publications of a computer-related crime scholar/researcher who has been retained to assist in profiling the computer felon(s) and determining modus operandi in a complex computer fraud case will be of direct relevance. Their availability could greatly assist the team by way of orientation, and such published views could be challenged if the technical advisor's identity is discoverable during pretrial.

What books or articles has the technical advisor written on the subject in question? Were they published, and if so, how recently? How were the expert's works received by his or her professional peers? Are the expert's works considered authoritative? Do other published works in the same field challenge or contradict the expert's published views? Are the expert's published views consistent in all of his or her writings? Are their [sic] published views, while consistent among themselves, congruent with the expert's current views espoused in the case at hand? These are all critical questions to be addressed when selecting an expert. Especially if there is to be an established or prolonged professional relationship with the expert, the initiative must be taken to analyze the consultant's published works and to later monitor the pretrial preparation process to avoid any significant discrepancies that may arise between present, planned testimony by the expert and past, possibly contradictory, positions he or she has taken.

Teaching and Other Consultancies

Activities that evidence a consultant's prior acceptance as an expert advisor or instructor go to the issue of their reliability and credibility as part of the government's team. Such activities as teaching or consulting in a given field are traditionally considered at the time an expert's credentials are presented to the court in preparation for taking the stand as an expert witness. Because of the newness and rapid evolution of computer-related technology, such credentials may hold more weight in a computer-related crime case than academic degrees or publications. A careful reference check with past consumers of the prospective expert's service—trainees or clients for whom they have consulted—can be an excellent way to assess that expert's reliability and stature, plus the currency and nature of his or her views, in advance of retention in a given case.

Extensive prior teaching and/or consultancies on the part of the government's expert can, if he or she has been retained for a fee, sometimes work to the detriment of the prosecution. For example, an expert who for a fee has done extensive training of investigators and prosecutors in the area of computer crime, and/or who has for a fee testified frequently for the prosecution in such cases, but not for the defense, could be impeached for bias and/or financial interest if called as an expert witness by the government.[2] Especially where a substantial percentage of an expert's income derives from such services to law enforcement, his or her comparative utility as an expert witness may be compromised.

Even if such an expert is not a potential expert witness, his or her identity and involvement in the preparatory stages of the case may prove discoverable by the defense and lead to allegations of bias in the technical advice rendered at the investigatory stage. These considerations aside, retention of an expert who has extensively trained and consulted for *only one side* in such cases can greatly lessen the fundamental value of having an outside expert on the investigative team to begin with.

Professional Associations

As in the case with professional licensure, certification or registration membership by a prospective expert in professional associations representing practitioners in the given subject is a credential which gives added weight to a presumption of competence and which is routinely included in the proffering of an expert's credentials to the court preparatory to the presentation of expert testimony. As with the matters of licensure, academic degrees, continuing education, and prior consultancies, membership in professional associations is subject to verification checks and to the gathering of references from the expert's professional peers. This is an important and useful quality control check which should always be taken advantage of, regardless of whether the technical advisor is viewed as a potential expert witness.

Previous Similar Experience

Due to the newness of the various computer technology fields and the speed with which new developments in computer technology are taking place, formal credentials are often of less importance in computer-related crime cases than is direct prior experience with the victim company's computer operations, the brands of hardware or software used by the victim, and the programming language involved. In addition, prior experience in investigating computer-related crimes, in providing computer security, or in computer-related crime research can be the critical element that renders a particular party an expert advisor. Identifying trustworthy and objective advisors who possess such direct prior experience can be the single most important aspect of selecting an expert. Despite the existence of traditional criteria, such as formal credentials, by which a proffered expert's qualifications to testify as an expert witness are normally assessed, the trial judge has broad discretion to base a decision that an individual is an expert qualified to testify on a given subject primarily - or even solely - on that person's prior relevant experience.

There are pitfalls in over reliance on technical advisors with extensive prior experience in the subject area. Maintaining control over the overall management and direction of the case can be one difficulty. Susceptibility to defense charges of partisanship and bias against experts with extensive prior experience which is disproportionately on the government's side only if such cases is another hazard. Regardless, this remains the single most important qualification to provide technical assistance in the ever-changing arena of computer-related crime.

Access to Privileged Information or Unique Facts

Employees of the victimized agency or of the manufacturer, vendor, or service organization whose computer products the victims utilized can be among the most useful of technical advisors when investigating a computer-related crime case or preparing one for trial. The backgrounds, education levels, and other credentials displayed by such persons can be expected to vary tremendously; this group will span top management at the victim organization, its in-house computer technologists, its data providers, equipment operators, and others who handle relevant data or are in possession of unique facts about the victim's operations. As a result qualifications for such persons in their respective fields, while important, will prove secondary to their familiarity with aspects of the victim's operations and equipment. For the narrow purpose of laying out what such operational practices routinely were or what equipment capabilities and vulnerabilities are, courts can be expected to admit expert testimony from such persons, provided the prosecution is able to demonstrate the expert witness's familiarity with such factors and his or her general competence.

The greatest pitfalls in the use of such individuals as pretrial technical advisors or as expert witnesses at trial obviously are: (1) distinguishing the true area of competence and (2) bias. Employees or service personnel may be qualified to speak authoritatively on only very narrow points and be completely unqualified on other related points. In addition, loyalty to the employer, job security considerations, or, on the other hand, a grudge against the employer or another employee may taint the individual's objectivity and hence utility. And, of course, the investigative team must be especially circumspect about bringing such persons in as technical advisors, unless and until their possible complicity in the crime has been completely ruled out.

Personal Qualities Of The Expert

Apart from credentials, the other primary set of standards against which must be measured the advisability of utilizing a given individual as a technical advisor or expert witness consists of the qualities of the prospective expert. Because this area is primarily subjective, as distinguished from the relative objectiveness of credentials, a presentation of what constitutes the key factors and how they should be assessed is difficult. However, eight generic considerations have been isolated which hold true for the use of technical advisors or expert witnesses in any major case, whether or not computer related. The following sections present these considerations.

Ability to Work as Part of a Team

Many individuals, regardless of the area of their professional competence, are not temperamentally or attitudinally geared to working as part of a team. Doubtless this problem is more prevalent with certain professions than with others due to the nature of the work performed and other factors. Assessing whether a prospective expert will be a team player is a critical decision that must be made at the earliest stage of the relationship, before the expert is retained. Reference checks and personal interviews are tools in making this determination. Effective management of the expert in the case, the security of sensitive investigative data, and the effectiveness of the expert as a witness on the stand are only a few of the overriding considerations that dictate utilizing only "team players" in expert roles.

Trustworthiness and Integrity

Despite the advisability of limiting a technical advisor's access to casework on a "need-to-know" basis, the expert will invariably be exposed to sensitive information during the course of the case. At the very least this will extend to a knowledge of his own role in the case, conversant with those aspects of the investigation where he or she has been providing input, and the identities of others on the investigative team. The trustworthiness and discretion of the expert must be assured and maintained.

As with the problem of insuring [sic] that the expert is a team player, detailed reference checks and personal interviews must be utilized to make a preliminary determination as to the expert's trustworthiness and integrity.

Professional Reputation and Recognition

A concomitant qualification to academic degrees and publications will be the notoriety of the expert and the professional reputation which he or she enjoys among their [sic] peers. While this will in part be a product of the authoritativeness of the expert's views and the prestigiousness of his or her formal credentials and experience in the field, it will also be reflective of the personal qualities which the expert displays. Many of the qualities will be directly relevant to whether the expert will be a good candidate for a harmonious working relationship with others on the case.

The expert's notoriety can cut both ways with regard to his or her credibility as an expert witness on the stand: If his or her views are controversial or even contested, the greater the expert's notoriety, the more likely the defense will be able to identify counterexperts familar with the views and at odds with them. On the other hand, increased notoriety can go to the issue of stature and authoritativeness, by which opposing expert opinion can be overshadowed.

Reference checks and a review of the literature in the field to accurately gauge an expert's professional stature and notoriety are important steps to be undertaken in advance of retention. Even if the expert is not to be retained as a potential expert witness, the nature of his or her role in the case or the nature of the retainer agreement can make the expert's identity discoverable by the defense at the pretrial stage, and thus open to attack his or her professional reputation and stature in the field.

Quality and Timeliness of Previous Work

It will be of critical importance to assess, in advance of retaining an expert, the quality of his previous work. Most directly, the quality of his or her prior consultancies and service as an expert witness must be checked out in great detail. In addition the general perception in the professional community as to the quality of the expert's work, publication, teaching, or lectures should be determined. If the government's expert is a potential expert witness, it can be assumed that the defense will make a thorough assessment in this area, and will attempt to impeach. The investigative and prosecutive team cannot afford surprises on cross-examination in this regard. Employers, prior clients, professional references, and professional and regulatory agencies, among others, should be contacted for an assessment of the quality and timeliness of the prospective expert's work.

Professional Bearing and Demeanor

Of perhaps subtle but always significant importance is the professional bearing and demeanor of the technical advisor. For potential expert witnesses the ability to speak authoritatively, to sustain composure under vigorous cross-examination, to avoid argumentativeness with opposing counsel, and to simplify for the judge and jury without condescension are essential characteristics to be displayed, the absence of any of which should screen the admitted expert out of the consideration as an expert witness. However these and other qualities must be present in the behind-the-scenes technical advisor, too, who must work closely with the other members of the investigative team, often under pressure.

Determining professional bearing and demeanor can be complicated. Initial impressions during interviews and preliminary discussions about the case are important, as are assessments by references and other outsiders. However all of these observations are of limited utility. Engaging in role-play early in the process with other investigators or prosecutors simulating an interrogation or cross·examination will display useful information about the expert's reactions under pressure and in response to challenges to his expertise. Playing devil's advocate in a discussion with the expert about his views or opinions on technical issues, or asking the expert to discuss the weaknesses in his own positions, or probing the expert on subjects beyond the area of expertise to assess the degree to which he or she is opinionated by nature are also useful techniques. In short, stress interviews for experts, whether or not they are viewed as potential expert witnesses, are an essential tool to gauge bearing and demeanor.

"Presence" Before a Group

The ability to effectively present ideas to a group is a learned skill. However, many individuals in all areas of endeavor lack this skill. An expert whose knowledge of a technical area is sound and who can effectively advise investigators behind the scenes may or may not possess an effective "presence" before a group.

This will be a critical skill in any expert witness; for potential expert witnesses, advance screening for the presence of this skill and practice sessions to enhance it for trial are a must. However, the ability to make effective presentations to groups may also be a necessary attribute of the behind-the-scenes technical advisor; this factor should be taken into consideration when retaining *any* expert.

Advisors at the investigative or pretrial stages of complex cases may be called upon to give orientation sessions on technical aspects of the case to a large group of investigators and other technical advisors. This will require the expert to be effective at group presentation. In addition should the identity of the technical advisor become known to the defense at the pretrial stage, depending on the nature of his relationship with the government and his role in the case, the expert may be subpoenaed to testify. This would require him to have the same ability to effectively command the attention of a group as if he had been designated as a potential expert witness by the government.

Articulation with Laymen

A thorough grounding in one's field of expertise and the ability to make an effective group presentation are undercut if a technical advisor is unable to simplify complex technical matters so that intelligent laymen can understand them. Indeed this is the most fundamental skill which a technical advisor or expert witness must possess. The ability to make technical points understandable to the members of the investigative or prosecutive team will be critical to their ability to erect a sound theory of the case and to implement an effective strategy to break the case and/or obtain a conviction. Similarly the ability to bring important technical points home to the judge and jury, without confusion or condescension, will directly impact on the likelihood of a favorable verdict.

If the expert has performed other consultancies in the past or served previously as an expert witness, determining whether he or she possesses this skill should prove easy by performing a thorough reference check. However, in the absence of these prior experiences, an effective technique would be to have the prospective expert explain to a group of lay office staff present in the office the meaning of a few technical terms or concepts selected by the interviewer. If the initiated observers cannot grasp the expert's explanation, chances are that other laypersons on the investigative team and on the jury will not readily understand either. The presence or absence of strong interpersonal communications skills in an expert is universally acknowledged as a key factor in the advisability of retaining him or her.

Mannerisms and Idiosyncracies

Distinctions distract. Peculiar mannerisms, unusual modes of dress, and other aspects of the expert's personality tend to deflect attention from the speaker's message to the speaker himself. The use of vulgarity or excessive humor at inappropriate times in a presentation of frequent ad hominen [sic] remarks about professional rivals would tend to alienate listeners against the speaker and thus against his message. Such distractions must be eliminated at all costs in the case of potential expert witnesses, either by behavior modification or replacement of the expert. Again, because behind-the-scenes technical advisors can under certain circumstances be subpoenaed to testify, these caveats are not limited to designated expert witnesses alone.

SOURCES FOR IDENTIFICATION OF INDIVIDUAL EXPERTS

Technical advisors for use in crime cases can be recommended by or drawn from a number of sources. These include the following:

1. In-house sources
2. Other law enforcement agencies
3. Other agencies of state or local government
4. State and local licensing, certifying, and registering bodies
5. Law enforcement professional associations
6. Professional associations in the subject area of expert knowledge sought
7. The victimized organization
8. The manufacturers/vendors and serving organizations who supply equipment or interface services to the victim
9. Other organizations in the victim's field of activity or industry
10. Area universities and research centers
11. Private consulting firms specializing in the subject area. Determining which source(s) to go to for a particular sort of expert will be dictated by a mix of factors [Exhibit Appendix.1]
12. Prior experience at obtaining experts
13. Available financial resources
14. Preexisting relationships with other agencies and referral sources
15. The facts and circumstances of each case

TYPES OF EXPERTS REQUIRED	IN-HOUSE RESOURCES	OTHER AGENCIES OF GOVERNMENT	LICENSING BODIES	PROFESSIONAL ASSN'S IN SUBJECT AREA	LAW ENFORCEMENT PROFESSIONAL ASSN'S	VICTIM COMPANY OR ORGANIZATION	HW/SW MANUFACTURER VENDOR/SERVICERS	OTHER ORGANIZATIONS IN VICTIM'S INDUSTRY	AREA UNIVERSITIES, RESEARCH CENTERS	PRIVATE CONSULTING FIRMS	OTHER LAW ENFORCEMENT AGENCIES
COMPUTER SCIENTISTS		X	X	X		X	X	X	X	X	
ELECTRONIC ENGINEERS		X	X	X		X	X	X	X	X	
TELECOMMUNICATIONS ENGINEERS		X	X	X		X	X	X	X	X	
COMPUTER CRIME SCHOLARS			X	X	X				X	X	X
SUBJECT MATTER EXPERTS FROM VICTIM'S INDUSTRY					X	X	X	X			
COMPUTER USERS						X	X	X			
DATA PROVIDERS						X	X	X			
COMPUTER OPERATORS						X	X	X			
NON COMPUTER PERSONNEL WHO INTERFACE IN VICTIM'S OPERATION						X	X	X			
EDP PROGRAMMERS	X	X	X	X	X	X	X	X	X	X	X
SYSTEMS ANALYSTS	X	X	X	X	X	X	X	X	X	X	X
DATABASE MANAGERS				X		X	X	X			
EDP AUDITORS	X	X	X	X	X	X	X	X	X	X	X
COMPUTER-SECURITY SPECIALISTS	X	X	X	X	X	X	X	X	X	X	X
EXPERIENCED COMPUTER-RELATED CRIME INVESTIGATORS	X	X	X	X	X		X		X		
FORENSIC SCIENTISTS	X	X	X	X	X		X		X		X

APPENDIX I. Likely sources of technical advisors in computer-related crime cases by type of experience required.

DISTINGUISHING THE TRUE AREA OF COMPETENCE

A concluding consideration when selecting an expert is offered as a caveat: Be certain of precisely what area(s) of expertise the investigative team needs to tap other advisors for, and be careful to distinguish between these various areas of technical expertise when selecting a given consultant. For example the decision to retain an EDP programmer, an EDP auditor, and a computer-security specialist as a core team of outside technical advisors when undertaking a complex computer related crime case will be a frequent decision. However, selecting a programmer who is proficient in the programming language of the victimized company will be equally essential. Selecting a programmer and an EDP auditor who are familiar with business applications of computer technology within the victim's field or industry will be a necessary distinction. When selecting a computer-security consultant, the need for a physical-security specialist, or a data-security specialist, or both must be discerned. (Most computer-security consultants are not expert at both aspects.) These examples could be expanded almost indefinitely.

Distinguishing the area(s) of specialized expertise needed must be coupled with distinguishing the true area(s) of a given consultant's expert competence from other areas in which he or she is not truly expert. This process is made more difficult because experts in one area are often unaware, or unwilling to admit, the limitations of their expertise. In situations such as these, reliance on representatives of the victimized organization or the manufacturers or vendors of the computer hardware or software equipment involved in the crime can be the best sources of guidance as to precisely what outside expertise is needed and what types of persons would be likely to possess the requisite capabilities. Consultation with experienced computer crime investigators or prosecutors, whether locally or from other jurisdictions, can be expected to be helpful on the more legal-related aspects of securing outside technical advice.

REFERENCES

1. J.D. Kogan, "On Being a Good Expert Witness in a Criminal Case," *Journal of Forensic Science*, (January, 1978), p. 195.
2. Michael H. Graham, "Impeaching the Professional Expert Witness by a Showing of Financial Interest," 53 Ind. L.J. 35, 44–47 (Winter 1977), p. 198.

APPENDIX II

CORRUPT CAPERS IN THE CHICKEN BUSINESS

After fathering six children and completing 14 years of employment with a variety of federal law enforcement and regulatory agencies with whom I had served in audit, compliance, investigative, and supervisory capacities, I fell prey to the need to earn more money. So I accepted an executive position with a new fast-food chain in Nashville, Tennessee, then called Minnie Pearl Chicken Systems, Inc. The company bore the name of that great lady of Grand Ole Opry fame, but she herself was only a small stockholder and inactive in day-to-day management. The year was 1969, and any celebrity with national name recognition was in the fast-food business. But that's another story.

I was given the job of managing a company division called Nashco Equipment and Supply. Nashco was organized as a profit center. It supplied both company-owned and franchised restaurants with restaurant decor, furniture, cooking equipment and utensils, uniforms, signage, and ad specialties. Nashco's operations were located about a mile from corporate headquarters in a leased warehouse and office facility of some 60,000 square feet. Nashco's major functional components at that site included purchasing, inventory control, sales, and physical distribution.

Nashco's physical distribution function included warehousing, receiving, and shipping activities. The latter included a fleet of leased trucks used to deliver restaurant equipment, supplies, and certain construction materials to new restaurant sites throughout the United States and Canada.

On the day I arrived to take over the division, the president of the company briefed me on his expectations. In simple terms his demand was, "Make money." He didn't say "or else." But I instinctively knew the implications. I inferred that because he made it clear that the division had *lost* money the year before—about $500,000.

The profit-center manager who had incurred the loss was still employed by the company. In fact he had been demoted and made an assistant—to me! However, the president suggested I could terminate him at any time, if I so desired.

It seemed to me that terminating the poor man should have been handled by someone either above me or by the corporate personnel director. At any rate I was stuck with him for the time being, mainly because I didn't know what else to do.

When I did meet my assistant, he seemed like a pleasant-enough chap. His previous experience and his education were in aeronautical engineering—a little odd perhaps, but we *were* in the *fast*-food business. So I didn't give it much further thought. Why should I? What did *I* know about the restaurant business? I was as green as he was—greener! He had been with the company for nine months.

My first day on the job, after my "executive briefing" with the president, was spent meeting all the members of my staff. Most of these folks were also relatively new at their jobs and showed evidence of insecurity in their roles. The only people who seemed secure in job roles were the warehousing people—stevedores, truck drivers, and the traffic manager. They at least knew their jobs and their place. They even showed great deference to me when I met them. But I didn't know why. (Was it typical of Southern culture to show deference for the boss? Perhaps. But here it seemed more than just deference. They almost feigned servility when I met them.)

As it turned out these were no gentlemen of the South. They were crooks. The evidence of their scams began to surface after I had had enough time to become better educated in my job. I spent my first two months learning as much as I could about the fast-food industry, franchising restaurant layouts and designs, and restaurant equipment purchasing and sales. I finally moved through the area I knew least and began to concentrate on what I knew best—accounting, finance, audits, controls, investigations, management, and security.

My first effort to reverse the previous year's loss was to review the previous year's operating statements and search for causes. Two items glared at me. Cost of sales was out of line the year before because of a large inventory shrink. Inventory per books was $200,000 higher than the physical count had indicated. The variance was about 10 percent—far more than anyone had expected. But nothing had been done to investigate the loss. The outside auditors made the appropriate adjustments, and the matter was left at that.

Another item was the high cost of transportation expense. I divided the total cost of transportation by the number of miles Ryder Truck Systems had billed us during the previous year. The resultant cost per mile was about double the national average for that time period.

So I had two things to work on now that I was freed from learning how to run a fried-chicken restaurant.

The inventory control group that reported to me consisted of three young ladies, two recent high school graduates and a supervisor, a woman of about 25 who appeared bright and hard-working.

One day when things seemed quiet (which wasn't very often in the halcyon days of fast food in Nashville in 1969), I visited with the inventory control supervisor and asked that she give me a briefing on what she and her crew did. She explained the manually kept perpetual inventory control system to me as best she could, after apologizing that she really was neither an accountant nor an auditor. She said she took a year of high school bookkeeping and had worked in the office of a moving company for several years before we hired her. At Minnie Pearl her training consisted of a four-hour briefing given by a member of the controller's staff. She apologized for the condition of the inventory records, saying there was more work than she and her staff could handle on a timely basis. So she often had to work overtime to catch up (for which she said she was not paid).

A cursory review of her in-process work and a few inventory ledger cards made my knees feel weak. She had not yet entered shipments of goods made three weeks earlier. And her recording of inbound merchandise was about equally tardy. For all intents and purposes we had no real inventory control system. Some goods were received and shipped out two weeks before any entry was made on the appropriate inventory ledger card.

What was worse, I discovered that a number of ledger cards contained red-ink entries. She explained that the procedure was recommended by a member of the controller's staff who informed her she should make such an entry whenever she went to the warehouse to make a spot check of certain inventory items. She hadn't fully understood the rationale for cycle counting of selected items, so whenever she noted a discrepancy—the balance shown on the card disagreed with her count—she merely made a red-ink entry on whichever side of the card the discrepancy favored. But she never advised anyone of the discrepancy or investigated any farther, and she never reconciled her pluses and her minuses to determine whether she had a net or more or less. At the year-end however, she did total the minuses and pluses out, she said. But not during the working year.

On one such ledger card there was a succession of red-ink entries. The ledger card related to large electric chicken fryers that cost the company over $1,000 each. Each of our restaurants needed four fryers. I quickly tallied her pluses and minuses and found the minuses were ahead by some 40 units, or by over $40,000!

A little investigating showed that an equipment serviceman for the company occasionally called from the field and ordered a replacement fryer for one that was in such a state of disrepair it needed to be sent back to the manufacturer on a warranty-claim basis. The warehousemen, lacking any prohibiting instructions, accommodated him.

What the serviceman did in fact was repair the chicken fryer on site, and when the new one arrived he would tell the restaurant manager the warehouse erred, and he himself would return the fryer—no problem. However the fryer never got back to the warehouse. It ended up in his garage, which was filled with other company property as well— refrigerator cabinets, heated cabinets, and even a knocked down walk-in cooler.

As soon as it became apparent that something was wrong by way of the ledger card for chicken fryers, I began calling franchises and asking them whether anyone had offered to sell them chicken fryers at reduced prices. On the fifth call a franchisee mentioned that the serviceman had offered to sell him several fryers for a new restaurant at very "reasonable" prices. The serviceman told him the fryers were brand new and still in the manufacturer's carton.

"Sure enough and so they were," said the franchisee.

"Where did he say he got them?" I asked.

"He didn't say and I didn't ask him," said the franchisee. "But I know where he kept them."

"Where's that?" I asked.

"In his garage," he said.

Armed with the franchisee's statement and our garbled inventory card, we got a search warrant for the serviceman's garage. There we found a treasure trove of restaurant equipment and supplies that belonged to the company.

So first things first, we developed a real inventory control system and hired an experienced person to supervise the function.

Transportation costs were next on the agenda. Our transport costs were horrendous. I tried the "rant and rave" approach to reduce costs early on but saw no real reduction. After the theft matter had settled down, I tried to find why transportation costs were so high.

I found that our truck fleet, after making deliveries of restaurant equipment, deadheaded back to Nashville, bypassing equipment manufacturers along the route. I thought that was strange, so I talked to the traffic manager. He said it was illegal for us to pick up our own inbound freight, that we were not common carriers and restaurant equipment was not an exempt commodity like farm produce. Our ICC permits allowed us to handle our own goods only after title had passed to us, which he said occurred after we received them at our warehouse.

So I called several manufacturers who sold us equipment and asked whether we could pick up our equipment purchases at their plant sites with our own fleet. They each said they would accommodate us, but we should change our purchase orders to show FOB their plant sites so as to not run afoul of ICC regulations. Changing the shipment from FOB destination point to FOB origination point caused title to pass to us at their plant so we could haul our own merchandise back and thus save the freight-in charges.

Feeling buoyed by this cost-cutting discovery, I called in the traffic manager and told him to coordinate his driver's return trips with the purchasing director and to pick up our equipment along the routes back to Nashville.

A month went by. No real reduction in transportation costs. The traffic manager skirmished with the purchasing director whenever he was told to have a returning truck make a pickup.

Then information came our way that indicated our truck drivers were unhappy about the notation of return loads. It kept them on the road a day or two longer, and away from their wives and children—or so they claimed. At least four of our drivers sought union representation from the Teamsters, as did a half-dozen warehouse employees.

What I didn't fully grasp was that I was ruining something a lot of people had a financial stake in. The drivers didn't want to pick up chicken fryers in Dallas or stainless steel sinks in St. Louis on their way back from Los Angeles because they already had a load to carry. What they were carrying back to Nashville was head lettuce and other fresh fruits and vegetables from California.

Several things tripped up the scheme. The first was collect phone calls made by our drivers to the traffic manager from strange places in California, places where we had neither existing restaurants nor new ones under construction; for example, Salinas has been known for its head lettuce ever since William Saroyan and John Steinback made it famous for that.

The Salinas calls caught my attention first. But then when Bakersfield showed up (potatoes) and Ventura/Oxnard (oranges, lemons), I knew something strange was happening. We had no restaurants within miles of these places and they weren't exactly along the route back to Nashville from San Francisco and Los Angeles where we did have a large number of restaurants.

The strange calls piqued my curiosity, but they weren't evidence of anything yet. My next move was to review the expense claims submitted by the drivers after their returns. That had been the responsibility of my assistant. When I asked that he send the vouchers directly to me from then on, he seemed miffed, as though I had insulted his integrity. He said it was a Mickey Mouse chore, better left to him or the traffic manager who really knew how to check the excesses of truck drivers who crib on their expense vouchers. When I insisted, he pouted but agreed to send me the vouchers.

I then visited the controller's office at corporate headquarters and asked to see all documentation that supported truck driver expense reports for the preceding six months.

In reviewing the documents submitted by drivers, I noted a recurring oddity. Weight statements at entry points on the Arizona border coming in from California seemed to be smudged, erased, written over, or just plain undecipherable. I selected about a half-dozen examples, made copies of the statements, and returned to my office. I then sent copies to a friend who was an Arizona state trooper, and asked him to secure for me copies of the state's own originals of the weight slips. Sure enough, when I got them back, the weights written on our copies were 20,000 or more pounds lower, indicating that the truck was loaded with *something* on its way back home.

Next we made phone calls to the numbers in Salinas, Oxnard, and Bakersfield. They were offices of product growers, merchants, and shippers. One claimed he sold lettuce to Minnie Pearl restaurants in Saint Louis. When told we had opened no restaurants in Saint Louis yet, he stammered and hung up.

We thought we could piece together what had happened at that point. But we needed confirmation. Our theory of the case was that the traffic manager through contacts with produce merchants in Nashville and Saint Louis and growers and shippers in California was doing a little moonlighting with our fleet.

Shipping fresh produce by rail or by truck from California is not cheap. But because the federal government has attempted to support agricultural economics by making special rules for farm products, such products are generally exempt commodities from the standpoint of certain ICC regulations. Truckers who haul farm products are subject to far fewer requirements and regulations. But because California ships out so much more produce than it takes in, its growers are chronically short of transportation mediums. So growers and shippers are eager to find any poor and lonesome trucker heading east with excess capacity. A thriving bootleg trucking business therefore existed that utilized the trucks of companies that could not find legitimate return loads.

The Minnie Pearl trucks were "sleepers" and carried two drivers so as to expedite deliveries and returns. The typical bootleg arrangement consisted of a $400 fee paid in cash to the two drivers by the grower or shipper. The drivers in turn took $100 each and gave $200 to our traffic manager who had brokered the deal to begin with.

We cracked the case by asking one pair of driver-partners to explain the discrepancy between the weight slips they had submitted with their expense vouchers and the originals of those slips that we had secured from the state of Arizona. They laid out the scheme and implicated other drivers and the traffic manager as the mastermind. Both confessed mainly because they were on parole—a report of the incident to parole authorities might have caused them to complete their prison sentences.

The traffic manager then implicated several other managers in the company as deriving benefits from his scheme.

BIBLIOGRAPHY

BOOKS

Bequai, August. *White-Collar Crime: A Twentieth-Century Crisis*. Lexington, Mass.: D. C. Heath, 1979.

Bologna, Jack. "Computer Crime: Wave of the Future." Madison, Wis.: Journal of Assets Protection, 1981.

Bologna, Jack. *Corporate Fraud—The Basics of Prevention and Detection*. Stoneham, Mass.: Butterworths, Inc., 1984.

Carroll, John M. *Computer Security*. Los Angeles: Security World Publishing Co., 1977.

Comer, Michael. *Corporate Fraud*. New York: McGraw-Hill, 1977.

Davis, Keagle W., William C. Mair, and Donald R. Wood. *Computer Control and Audit*. Altamonte Springs, Fla.: Institute of Internal Auditors, Inc., 1976.

Elliott, Robert K., and John J. Willingham. *Management Fraud: Detection and Deterrence*. New York: Petrocelli Books, 1980.

Grau, J. J., and B. Jacobson. *Criminal and Civil Investigation Handbook*, New York: McGraw-Hill: 1981.

Hoyt, Douglas. *Computer Security Handbook*. New York: MacMillan Publishing Company, Inc., 1973.

Katz, J. *Concerted Ignorance, The Social Construction of Cover-Up.* Washington, D.C.: U.S. Department of Justice Law Enforcement Assistance Administration, 1979.

Kell, William G., and Robert K. Mautz. *Internal Controls in U.S. Corporations.* New York: Financial Executives Institute Research Foundation, 1980.

Kirk, Paul L., and John I. Thornton, Eds. *Crime Investigation* 2d ed. New York: John Wiley & Sons, 1974.

Klotter, John C. *Criminal Evidence,* Cincinnati: Anderson Publishing Co., 1980.

Koba Associates, Inc. *Expert Witness Manual: Use of Outside Experts in Computer-Related Crime Cases,* Washington, DC: U.S. Department of Justice, 1980.

Krauss, Leonard I., and Aileen MacGahan. *Computer Fraud and Countermeasures.* Englewood Cliffs, N.J.: Prentice-Hall, 1979.

O'Hara, Charles E. *Fundamentals of Criminal Investigation.* 3d ed., Springfield, Ill: Charles C. Thomas, 1978.

Osborn, Albert S. *Questioned Document Problems.* Albany, N.Y.: Boyd Printing Co., 1944.

Parker, Donn B. *Crime by Computer* New York: Charles Scribner's Sons, 1976.

Russell, Harold F. *Foozles and Frauds.* Altamonte Springs, Fla.: Institute of Internal Auditors, 1977.

Schabeck, Tim. *Computer Crime Investigation Manual.* Madison, Wis: Journal of Assets Protection, 1979.

Treasury Department. *Financial Investigative Techniques* Washington, DC: Internal Revenue Service, 1979.

Vaughan, D. *Controlling Unlawful Organizational Behavior—Social Structure and Corporate Misconduct.* Chicago: University of Chicago Press, 1983.

Wagner, Charles. *The CPA and Computer Fraud.* Lexington, MA: Lexington Books, 1979.

ARTICLES

Allen, Brandt R. "Embezzler's Guide to the Computer. "*Harvard Business Review* 53, no. 4, (1975): 79

Allen, Brandt R. "Computer Fraud." *Financial Executive* 39 (May 1971): 38-43

Bailey, J. "What Is the Internal Auditor's Role?—Fraud Investigation." *Internal Auditor* 35, no. 2 (April 1978): 7

Baker, D. W., M. J. Barrett, and L. R. Radde "Top-Management-Fraud—Something Can Be Done Now!" *Internal Auditor* 33, no. 5, (October 1976): 9

Carmichael, D. R. "What is the Independent Auditor's Responsibility for the Detection of Fraud?" *Journal of Accountancy* 140, no. 5, (November 1975): 76–80

Cherrington, D. J., W. S. Albrecht, and M. B. Romney. "Role of Management in

Reducing Fraud—Corporate Responsibility." *Financial Executive* 49, no. 3, (March 1981): 28–32, 34

Gale, C. "Stamp Out Fraud—Clue for Detecting Insurance Fraud." *Security Management* 25, no. 10, (October 1981): 57–61

Gates, P. O. "How Can Accountants and Auditors Prevent Computer Fraud?" *Government Accountants Journal* 27, no. 2, (Summer 1978): 10–15

Graham, Michael H. "Impeaching the Professional Expert Witness by a Showing of Financial Interest." *Indiana Law Journal* 53, (1975): 35

Kapnick, H. "Responsibility and Detection in Management Fraud" *CPA Journal* 46, no. 5 (May 1976): 19–23

"Management Fraud—Preventive Actions for Business." Coopers & Lybrand Newsletter 19, no. 4, (April 1977): 7

Pomeranz, F., and A. J. Cancellieri. "Management Fraud—What Business Can Do for Itself." *Financial Executive* 45 (September 1977): 18–23

Romney, M. "Detection and Deterrence—A Double-Barreled Attack on Computer Fraud." *Financial Executive* 45, no. 7, (July 1977): 36–41

Ross, I. "How Lawless Are Big Companies?" *Fortune* (December 1, 1980) 56—64

Russell, H. F. "Facing the Problem." *Internal Auditor* 932, no. 4, (July/August 1975): 13–22

Sawyer, L. B., and A. A. Murphy. "Management Fraud—the Insidious Specter." *Journal of Assets Protection* 4, no. 2 (May/June 1979): 13–20

Shaw, Paul, D. "Investigative Accounting." *Journal of Assets Protection* 3, no. 1 (Spring 1978)

Sommer, A. A., Jr. "Disclosure of Management Fraud." *Business Lawyer* 31 (March 1976): 1283–1293

Vandiver, James V. "Forensic References." *Journal of Assets Protection* 2, no. 4 (Winter 1977)

INDEX